From Worst to First

The Toronto Blue Jays in 1985

From Worst to First

The Toronto Blue Jays in 1985

by Buck Martinez

Fitzhenry & Whiteside Limited
Toronto

From Worst to First
The Toronto Blue Jays in 1985

Fitzhenry & Whiteside Limited
195 Allstate Parkway
Markham, Ontario L3R 4T8

Designer   *Sandi Meland/Word & Image*
Typesetting by   *Jay Tee Graphics Ltd.*
Printed and bound in Canada by   *Gagné Printing*
Cover photograph   *Canada Wide/The Toronto Sun / Stan Behal*

Facts and figures within the Statistics Appendix
of this book have been assembled and supplied courtesy
the Toronto Blue Jays Ball Club.

Canadian Cataloguing in Publication Data

Martinez, Buck, 1948 -
 From worst to first

ISBN 0-88902-913-X

1. Toronto Blue Jays (Baseball team).
2. Martinez, Buck, 1948-   3. Baseball
players - Biography. I. Title.

GV875.T6M37 1985   796.357'64'09713541   C85-090838-8

Contents

1   Spring Training   1
2   A Critical Look at the Pitchers   7
3   The Blue Jay Players   25
4   The Season Begins   40
5   Toronto 2, Detroit 0
     June 6, 1985   54
6   Mid-Season Pain and Triumphs   59
7   Out at Home   69
8   The Mighty Fallen   81
9   Spoilers   92
10   Clinching the Pennant   97
11   Dave Stieb   114
12   The American League Championship
     Series   119
13   Bobby Cox and Jimy Williams   139
14   Martinez on Martinez   146
     Statistics   159

Dedication

In a game that encourages men to be boys, so many of us get caught up in the fleeting excitement of our successes only to find they are empty and short-lived. There is only one thing that lasts — the love of your wife and family. They will survive the 0 for fours, the errors and the losses. They will be there beyond the basehits and shutouts and beyond the cheers and autograph seekers.

Without Arlene's love and support, intelligence and integrity there would have never been an opportunity for this book. She simply asked me to be myself for myself. Because of that I'm proud to dedicate this book to her and to our son, Casey.

From Worst to First

The Toronto Blue Jays in 1985

photograph by Neal Sadja

CHAPTER 1

Spring Training

"FIRST OF ALL, I'D LIKE TO WELCOME YOU ALL TO CAMP, AND tell you all how happy I am to have you here. We, the front-office personnel, the coaches and myself, feel that this is the best team this club has ever put together, and, if we all work hard here in Florida, we'll leave camp with a club good enough to win our division. I haven't yet made up my mind as to who will make the team, but rest assured we'll be taking a good look at all of you, and everyone will get a chance to play . . . to show us what you can do."

The rookies are all ears.

I've heard that speech a dozen times: from Charlie Metro, Bob Lemon, Jack McKeon, Whitey Herzog in Kansas City, George Bamburger with the Brewers and, finally, from Bobby Cox with the Blue Jays.

It's always pretty much the same.

For the new boys, it has to be exciting. This is their first day in the sun. They dream of making diving catches to save the game, or hitting that ninth-inning homer to win it for the home team. They conjure up late-inning relief appearances against the Phillies that might make the difference between a trip to Kansas City for an opener or a trip to Cecil Englebert's Minor League complex, and destinations unknown: *Syracuse . . . Knoxville . . . Kinston . . . or beyond.*

There are also the journeymen, players who have been around, who are on the down sides of their careers, and are hoping to land that 24th or 25th spot on yet another team.

It's the stuff of dreams: teenagers panting for a shot at the big leagues; veterans wondering if this might be the last trip south.

• • • •

Clubs that struggled through 1984, have made those changes that will bring the pennant home. Players who turned in bad years, call them *off years*, and hurry in to prove that off-season conditioning programs have turned them into number-one candidates for their old positions on the field.

For all clubs and for all players, it's a time of hope; the most promising time, in fact, of the baseball year. The sad fact of the matter, however, is that in my 16 years of spring training, I could always sit down with the team's new press guide and come within two players of naming the opening-day roster even before the first pitch was thrown.

That aside, in the spring of 1985, there was one dream, one excitement in which we all shared. We were all Toronto Blue Jays, about to step onto the field in those early days of what promised to be our best year yet.

There had been some very big deals over the winter months, deals that had all but cinched our winning the American League East. The season-long chase of the Tigers in 1984 had told us that while we were a pennant-class club, we were still a little short in the bullpen. Dennis Lamp, who had been acquired prior to the season was probably not best suited for the short role. In fact, he pitched much better in the spot starts, relief appearances and as middle relief. Roy Lee Jackson, one of the incumbents, had shown signs of brilliance during different periods of the season, but failed to give us the consistent performance we needed in a stopper. There was fairly unanimous agreement that to make it over the hump to a first division pennant, we needed help in the short corps.

Pat Gillick went to work.

In December, Oakland's ace, Bill Caudill, was acquired in a trade for shortstop Alfredo Griffin and outfielder Dave Collins. Caudill had saved 88 games over the past three seasons — 26 each in '82 and '83 with Seattle, and an impressive 36 with the As in '84.

The pieces began to fall in place, but was the price too high? I, for one, didn't think so.

Griffin had been a valuable part of our team. He never missed a game and gave us everything he had whenever he stepped onto the field. A solid shortstop with great range, his exuberance meant a lot to the players. He would be missed. Dave Collins was coming off a banner year for us, stealing bases at a record clip and batting over .300. Both Dave and Griff meant a lot to the team, and to individual players like Moseby, Garcia and Bell. Griff and Damo were a great double-play combination. Each seemed to know what the other was thinking every minute of the game; but watching young Tony Fernandez play, particularly late in the '84 season, you couldn't help thinking that one of our two shortstops would have to go. Dave's uncanny knowledge of the movement between opposing pitchers and first base was passed along to many members of the team, and was probably the main reason we became so adept at running other teams crazy. Yet, here again, with three young, budding stars in the outfield — Moseby, Bell and Barfield — Davie became expendable.

When I heard about these trades back home in Kansas, I thought we finally had all the pieces we needed to make a run at the pennant. What I didn't know was that Pat had not yet finished moulding his team — not by a long shot.

Again he was on the phone, this time with the San Francisco Giants looking for left-handed help, and in January the announcement came that right-handed starter, Jim Gott, two minor league pitchers, Jack McKnight and shortstop Augie Schmidt, had been dealt to the Giants for Gary Lavelle. Another veteran stopper with great credentials! Things were looking better all the time.

Pudge Lavelle had run up great numbers over his ten-year stand with the Giants. He had set a club mark with 127 saves in 647 games, passing Hall of Fame great Christie Matthewson. All of a sudden, we had gone from having good young arms with promise to having those same young arms plus two proven short men to back them up.

You have to give something to get something, they say in

baseball; in this case, while we had definitely given up some fine ball players, we got exactly what we needed in return.

I could hardly wait to get to work. Even with the Tigers being in our division, many sports writers had picked us to be the best team in baseball.

Had we come this far already?

It seems we had.

• • • •

The routine of spring training is very repetitive; year after year, day after day, it's always the same. Pitchers and catchers report a week ahead of time — pitchers to get in shape by throwing batting practice to the regular players; catchers to be there to catch pitchers so they can get into shape to throw batting practice to the regulars. so, as strange as it might seem, the first week of spring training for a catcher is probably harder than any other time of the year. All he's doing is catching.

Most teams, and the Blue Jays are no different, bring extra catchers to spring training to try to give their regular catchers a break and not wear out anybody.

We took three young catchers to camp in 1985: Jeff Dewillis, Jeff Hearron and Dave Stenhouse. We also picked up Gary Allenson right before spring training began. Despite the regimen, despite the grunts and groans, spring training is a fun time. We start out daily with a jog around the field, then do a 20-minute exercise routine. This is the relaxing part of the day because it gives players a time to renew old acquaintances, to stand out in the sun and stretch and to exchange barbs and ribs with teammates.

There are always jokes about Doyle Alexander's age: how did he ever make it through the winter, as old as he is? There is a lot of talk about Acker and his deerhunting, and whether or not he got arrested down in Texas for jumping over fences. And so on. . .

There are the introductions to the new people and, always, on the first day of camp, Bobby Cox's meeting at which everybody is required to step onto the scales and weigh in. The club sends a letter during the winter, asking each player to report at a particular weight. The spring-training weight (decided by the club) is designed to keep each individual at his best, from Day One throughout the long season. This is the weight that will allow each player to maximize his strength and be in the best shape possible. In 1985, everyone weighed in at the proper weight, or close to it, except for three guys.

Everybody kids Ernie Whitt about his appetite for doughnuts. Jokes fly around the clubhouse on the mornings of day games. Whenever anybody reaches for a doughnut, we say, "Oh, you better ask Ernie," or "Check with Ernie, they're his." Sure enough, Ernie weighed in a little bit overweight, nothing serious.

Bill Caudill, new to the team, was also overweight, and so was Roy Lee Jackson. Naturally, Bobby Cox said he'd like to talk to each of them after that first practice. Just as naturally, mysterious signs suddenly appeared over both Ernie's and Caudill's lockers.

Caudill's sign read *"Tubby 1,"* and Ernie's was *"Tubby 2"*. These precipitated a lot of fake anger and clubhouse ranting and raving. Lots of warnings were issued and lots of threats. "Whoever did this . . . I'll get even with you guys! Don't ever do that again!" The signs stayed up. Neither Caudill nor Ernie even attempted to take them down. They were part of the good-natured ribbing that goes on in a unified ball club.

Caudill has always been noted for his pranks and for his ability to keep a team loose. When he was in Seattle and the team had done badly and there was really not an awful lot to laugh about, Billy felt it was his responsibility to keep the club up. He was nicknamed "Cuffs" because he frequently carried handcuffs which he'd use to cuff his teammates to the dugout or the fence near the bullpen. He was also named "The Inspector". He would walk out onto the field wearing his Sherlock Holmes hat and puffing on his long Meerschaum pipe, and snoop around trying to find those Mariners' bats that had mysteriously disappeared. In the spring of 1985, we didn't really know Caudill but we felt, because of his reputation, we could also join in the fun.

John Sullivan, the bullpen coach, and Jim Acker, always eager for a little levity, were sitting in the bullpen one day before a game, watching Caudill, when Sully decided to put a tag on him — "Sid." Sully was really enjoying it, chuckling to himself, thinking he had really done something. This bugged my curiosity no end, so I said, "Sid . . . Sid . . . who's Sid? What does it mean?" Sully whispered to me, "Sid Fernandez."

Sid Fernandez is a left-handed pitcher for the New York Mets. He's a very good pitcher, but at the start of spring training in '85 he was somewhat rotund. He probably weighed in at about 250 or 260. Billy weighs probably 210, maybe even less than that, and he is in pretty good shape. Nevertheless, Sully had put a bug in my ear and, naturally, knowing that Caudill was going to pitch in the ninth inning, I had to do something. I spied Howie Starkman walking from the clubhouse behind the bleachers and I jumped to my feet. I ran over to him. "Howie, you've got to do me a favor."

"What?"

I asked him if, when Caudill came out to pitch the ninth inning, he would introduce him as "Sid" Caudill.

Howie laughed when I told him the significance of the moniker but said, "I can't do that — Caudill will blame me. He'll crucify me."

"Don't worry about it. He'll never find out."

The next inning, when Caudill went up to the mound, Howie Starkman made the announcement: "Now pitching for the Toronto Blue Jays — Sid Caudill!" There was a muted chuckle throughout the stands, even though nobody really understood what it meant. Down in the bullpen, I was biting my lip until it was about ready to bleed. Sully and Acker turned in opposite directions and acted as if nothing had happened. We looked out of the corners of our eyes, down at the mound, where Caudill was perched.

He had his hands placed squarely on his hips and was staring directly at the bullpen, at Sully, Jim Acker, and myself. I knew we were in a heap of trouble, but Oh, was it worth it!

After the game, Bill said, "Now you've done it! You've embarrassed me in front of my wife and my mother. I'll get you guys. I'll get you!" We knew he really would, but it *was* so funny.

That's the kind of spirit Billy Caudill brings to a club.

He's very loose, and he's happy to be on a new team. We're eager for him to be here. He enjoys himself out on the field and he shows it. He gives baseball his all, and the players make good use of his spirit. He's a great addition to this ball club.

CHAPTER 2

A Critical Look at the Pitchers

A SAMPLING OF PITCHERS TRAINING FOR THE 1985 TORONTO Blue Jays Ball Club at spring training in Dunedin, Florida included:

JIM ACKER, 26 years old, 6 ft, 2 in. tall, 212 lbs, right-handed pitcher. Jim had two years of major league service, and was acquired from the Atlanta Braves through the major league draft on December 6, 1982. Jimmy has a sinker ball, a slider and a change-up. He has such outstanding stuff that many opposing batters around the American League accuse him of throwing a spit ball. One of my former team mates, Al Cowens, who is now playing with the Seattle Mariners, swears that Jim throws a spit ball and has told me: "Buck, you can't tell me that that's not a spitter. No one throws a sinker ball that hard that sinks that well. Acker is simply unhittable. There's no way that that can NOT be a spitter."

In 1985, Jimmy really needed a good spring training. The competition on our ball club is so keen that Jim knew before he even started the spring that he would have to battle for a spot on the ten-man staff. He is valuable, in my mind, because he can do many things. He can spot-start; he can pitch middle relief; and he can pitch short relief. Jim's ability to pitch several days in a row is important. I think Coxie likes

Gary Lavelle, Jim Acker and Bill Caudill

him because of his attitude. Jim is a "give me the ball; I'll do the best I can; and see what happens" pitcher. He's a tremendous competitor on the mound.

Jim needs to get his control down so that he can go "strike one" on the batter. If he pitches ahead using his good sinker ball, and keeps ahead of the batters, then he can utilize his knuckle-curve ball and the change-up to mow down the opposition. Jim has had trouble in the past when he fell behind in the count and had to come in with his sinker ball. It's an outstanding pitch, but not one to use all the time.

DOYLE ALEXANDER, 35 years old, 6 ft, 3 in., 200 lbs, right-handed pitcher. Doyle has thirteen years of major league experience. When he was released by the New York Yankees on June 1, 1983, Bobby Cox was immediately alert because they had worked together in 1982 with the Atlanta Braves; Coxie felt then that Doyle was a good pitcher. Coxie asked me in 1983 what I thought about Doyle, and I told him, quite frankly, that I didn't think he could help the club. I thought his best years were behind him. He didn't look as if he was popping the ball. We had seen him the previous spring in New Orleans during an exhibition game when he was pitching with the Yankees, and I just didn't think he had the velocity. Coxie told me, "Wait till you catch him. You'll like the way he pitches. He's an outstanding pitcher. He has good knowledge of the game, and he throws a lot of strikes." Coxie went ahead to sign Doyle for the Blue Jays.

Alexander was sent to Kingston in A-ball to get in shape and start again. He was recalled to Toronto on August 1.

Doyle is a difficult guy to learn how to catch; he has a fast ball, a slider, and a change-up, and he throws from several different deliveries. The toughest thing for me to get comfortable with was Doyle's tremendous confidence in his change-up. He feels he can throw it at any time. It is definitely one of the best change-ups in all of baseball.

I sure was wrong about Doyle and I've told him the story several times. He is a very valuable person to have on this ball team. I love the way he sets up hitters. He's a tremendous student of the opposition's batters. He sits on the bench every game when he's not pitching and religiously watches how the hitters react to certain pitches thrown by our staff. When I have any trouble with the hitters, I go to Doyle and ask him "How do we pitch this guy? What are we doing

9

photograph by Dan Hamilton

Doyle Alexander

wrong? Can you help me out?'' I know that Doyle knows; he always pays attention. He knows what the opposition is hitting and he always knows how to get them out. Doyle has been a tremendous help to me personally in learning how to pitch and constantly in learning how to utilize our pitching staff. His experience lends a lot to our staff, because he has been through pennant races and he has been in the World Series.

Doyle has gotten more out of his ability than anyone I've ever seen in the game. He's not blessed with the overpowering stuff of a Stieb, or a Clancy, but he does have a tremendous desire to excel. I don't think there is anyone who works as hard as Doyle does in between starts, trying to perfect his motion and his control to the point where he can pinpoint his pitches. Doyle can pop some fast balls up to 87-88 miles an hour. His outstanding control and his very, very sharp use of the change-up, however, make a devastating combination.

Doyle did not have to do an awful lot during spring training. He needed to go out, get in shape, make sure his arm was sound, work on his control and the command of his pitches. He knew what he had to do to win. You don't have to tell Doyle much. I'm sure that in his mind he knew exactly where he wanted to be by the end of spring training. I don't think that anyone doubted that Doyle Alexander would be ready for the 1985 season.

BILL CAUDILL, right-handed pitcher, 28 years old, 6 ft, 1 in. tall, 210 lbs. As I mentioned earlier, Bill was acquired from the Oakland As in a trade for Dave Collins and Alfredo Griffin on December 8, 1984. He is a short-relief pitcher who has had tremendous success over the last three years.

Billy is basically a one-pitch pitcher. He's got an outstanding fast ball, which he throws in a 90-mile-an-hour range, and he relies on good control. He needs to keep his fast-ball velocity up in spring training. I'm certain that all Billy has to do is throw a lot in the spring; he should pitch on a regular rotation or get a lot of save and short-inning situations so that he can be ready to peak towards the end of training. Billy is a power pitcher, so he takes a little bit longer than a controlled pitcher to develop his arm strength, to get it back into season form after the long winter layoff. After seeing him perform

11

Jim Clancy

12

for the last couple of years, I know he's got a lot of enthusiasm and a lot of competitiveness.

JIM CLANCY, 29-year-old right-hander, 6 ft, 4 in. tall, 220 lbs. Jim has got seven years of major league experience, all with the Toronto Blue Jays. He was selected from the Texas Rangers, November 5, 1976 in the expansion draft. He is one of three original Blue Jays remaining on the team.

Since 1980, Jimmy has started 136 games, rarely missing a start. He really is a workhorse on the staff, always throwing well over 200 innings. Clancy is a true power pitcher, possessing a 90-mile-an-hour fast ball, and a great breaking slider.

What Jimmy needs is to be more consistent; he needs good control so that he can throw his fast ball over the plate at any time and stay ahead of the hitters. Another thing which I think that Al Widmar, the pitching coach, wanted Jimmy to do was to develop a good off-speed pitch. Jim has experimented in the past with a fork ball and several different kinds of change-ups, but has never really mastered any of these. I think one of Jim's goals in spring training was to come up with a reliable change-up. I feel he should combine a change-up with his outstanding fast ball and breaking slider. There aren't too many people who work as hard as Jim Clancy during spring training. He's always out there running his sprints, making sure he gets in a good workout. Jim is dedicated to throwing; he is always trying to come up with something new on his delivery.

JIMMY KEY, 23 years old, 6 ft, 1 in., 185 lbs, left-handed pitcher. Jimmy was obtained in the third round of the 1982 free-agent draft, out of Clemson University. After his first spring training in 1984, he showed a lot of promise, but was sent to the minor leagues as one of the last cuts. He showed unusual poise for a young pitcher that spring, and impressed everyone with his velocity and his ability to throw strikes. When Stan Clarke and Bryan Clark both showed control problems in the Vancouver series prior to opening day, Bobby Cox made a switch and recalled Jimmy Key. It was a good year for Jimmy. He set rookie records with 10 saves in 63 games and also made 63 relief appearances; both were club records.

Jimmy was used exclusively as a starting pitcher in his first two years in professional ball. While in Toronto in 1984 he

Jimmy Key

was used exclusively out of the bull pen because of the shortage of left-handers. Jimmy would make a good major league starter, and 1985 was his year to break into the rotation. Coxie used him as a fifth starter in Florida to see how he would do.

One thing I try to do as a catcher is to get my pitchers to pitch inside. Pitchers who can throw effectively inside to the batters take away the outside part of the plate and become much more effective opponents. Jimmy Key has the ability to throw good, hard fast balls to the inside part of the plate to right-handed hitters. He can then set up all his pitches to the outside part of the plate later on in a count. When a batter knows a pitcher can throw to both sides of the plate, he has to give up one side or the other, and cannot really sit on a particular pitch. Jimmy developed this ability early, something unusual in a young pitcher. He has outstanding fast balls that he can run into the right-handers; he has good, sinking fast balls that he can run away from them; he has a great, sharp, breaking curve ball, a fair slider and rapidly improving change-up. Jimmy Key is a solid, left-handed starter. His performance in Florida showed us that Jimmy could pitch well in the rotation. He was an important feature on the Blue Jays pitching staff in 1985.

GARY LAVELLE, 35 years old, 6 ft, 1 in., 200 lbs, left-handed reliever. Gary was obtained from the San Francisco Giants in a trade for Jim Gott, Jack McKnight, a minor league pitcher, and Augie Schmidt on January 26, 1985. During his ten years as a Giant, Gary compiled some impressive numbers, working out of the bull pen. He surpassed the great Hall of Famer Christie Matthewson for all-time records in saves at 127, in games 647. His consistent performance as a short man and his ability to overpower left-handers makes him a great right-handed complement to Bill Caudill in late-inning situations. We now have two experienced short relievers, a welcome surplus in an area that has been a problem for the club from its inception.

Gary has pitched recently for a perennial second division team; he should be very excited about the promising season ahead. I talked with several National Leaguers over the winter, and all of the hitters were pleased with the idea they would not be facing Pudge this season. I was told that he still had an outstanding fast ball and a nasty slider that gave both

15

Dennis Lamp

right- and left-handed hitters fits, and I looked forward to catching him. It was a learning process for all three of us — Gary, Ernie and myself. Gary needed to learn how Ernie and I catch and call a game; Ernie and I needed to learn Gary's style of pitching and to try to make his American League debut as comfortable as possible.

DENNIS LAMP, 32 years old, 6 ft, 3 in. 215 lbs, right-handed pitcher. Dennis was signed as a free agent on January 10, 1984. In 1983, he led the White Sox in 15 saves and really contributed a lot in the stretch on the White Sox' way to the playoffs.

Dennis got off to a fast start for the Blue Jays in 1984, gaining 8 of his 9 saves by May 23. Denny has a sinker ball and sets a lot of ground balls, but he ran into some control problems in the middle of the season. Signing as a free agent and coming to a new team, I feel Lampie put too much pressure on himself and tried to carry the whole load of the ball club on his shoulders as the "saviour" out of the bull pen. How many Goose Gossages or Rollie Fingers are there? Not too many. When Dennis struggled, he tried harder and things got worse. Bobby felt he might be better suited to starting, and an opportunity became available in Minnesota on August 27. Dennis relaxed on the mound and responded with a 5-2 victory. He went on to compile a 3-0 record with a 3.38 ERA as a starter. With renewed confidence and a relaxed attitude, he began to throw the same way he had done earlier; he found his most productive positions on the staff were those of middle reliever and spot starter.

In 1985, Dennis would play that same role, and, although he is the happy-go-lucky comedian of the club, my impression is that 1984 was a big letdown for him. Dennis has great pride and determination, and 1985 would be a much better year for him. He was used as the middleman to set up Caudill and Lavelle.

DAVE STIEB, 27 years old, 6 ft, 1 in., 195 lbs, right-handed pitcher. Dave was the Blue Jays' fifth-round draft pick in the 1978 free-agent draft, out of Southern Illinois University where he also played in the outfield. In 1981, he became the first Blue Jay pitcher to have a winning record at 11-10, and he has been a winning pitcher ever since. He has compiled a whopping 50-34 record. Blessed with a great arm, Dave was rushed through the system and, after only 19 games in the minor leagues, was promoted to the majors in 1979.

The year 1984 was outstanding for the California native with a 16-8 record and a 2.83 ERA, ranking him second behind league leader, Mike Boddicker. Dave is truly one of the overpowering pitchers in the league, with a great, moving fast ball and one of the best sliders that has ever been thrown by a major leaguer. He is still learning how to pitch to his point, relying mostly on sheer ability. As he watches and learns more about the art of mixing pitches, and learning hitters' weaknesses, Dave will actually get better. I don't think I've ever seen as intense a competitor take the mound. I feel Dave expects to be perfect each and every time he goes out there, and that simply does not happen with *any* athlete in any sport. The great pitchers, like Carlton, Seaver, Hunter and Gibson, weren't always on, but they had the knowledge and the ability to recognize that, and they pitched simply to beat the batter, not to embarrass him. Dave hasn't reached that point yet. He has the ability to win 20 games, but he has to lean how to control himself and to understand what it takes to be a bigger winner.

A successful pitcher is made up of the following:

— consistency, the ability to go in there day in and day out, ready to win;

— an awareness of hitters' reactions to pitches seen during an at bat;

— an ability to recognize the weaknesses of each batter and to take advantage of those weaknesses;

— an awareness of where the game is going — the score, who's on deck, when to go for the strikeout, when to go for the ground ball;

— an acceptance of the fact that batters will get hits, coupled with a strategy for closing out a team with double plays and ground balls.

There is more to pitching than throwing good pitches three times in a row and striking out the batter. Winning is managing the pitches, by consistently pitching seven, eight, nine innings of good, solid baseball. A good pitcher will always keep his team in a winning position. Great pitchers are winners. They win without always being hot.

Dave Stieb will be a great pitcher. He gets closer every time he goes to the mound. He is learning more about Dave Stieb, the pitcher, each time he's on the field — what he is capable of doing, and what he is not capable of doing on a particular day.

Pitching is very difficult, and great pitchers learn and learn and learn. They never stop learning. This spring was not so different for Dave Stieb. He was ahead of everyone else by a week. He threw well the first day off the mound. His first exhibition outing was close to mid-season form. The idea of Stieb not being ready to open the season had never entered anyone's mind. He worked hard; he was ready for the season, and he was the opening day pitcher in Kansas City on April 8. No one had to tell Dave Stieb what to do.

LUIS LEAL, 27 years old, 6 ft, 3 in., 220 lbs, right-handed pitcher. Louie signed as free agent on November 24, 1978. 1985 was Louie's fourth year in Toronto as a regular in the rotation, compiling a 35-28 record over that time. He got off to a great start in '84, going 6-0 before losing to the Detroit Tigers on June 6. By All-Star break, he was 9-2 with a solid 3.0 ERA. Many of us on the team felt he should be named to the all-star team, but he failed to be selected. The second half wasn't quite as good to Louie; he fell to 4-6; but 1984 was still his best major league season to date, at 13-8.

This spring, Louie had a different approach to training camp, because he did not pitch winter ball for his hometown team, the Barquisimetro Cardinales in Venezuela. I was not too concerned, because Louie has a very sound arm, and would actually benefit from the layoff. He started as the fourth starter behind Stieb, Clancy and Alexander. Leal has a good fast ball and a slider and occasionally throws a curve ball. Pitching coach, Al Widmar, tried to work on Leal's change-up during spring training so as to include that in his repertoire.

RON MUSSELMAN, 30 years old, 6 ft, 2 in., 185 lbs., right-handed pitcher. Ronnie was purchased from the Syracuse Chiefs August 16, 1984, after he started the season with the Texas Rangers' Triple-A Club in Oklahoma City. At Syracuse, he was 1-2, with 8 saves in 26 games. During the last month and a half spent in a Blue Jay uniform in 1984, he was 0-2 with a fine 2.11 ERA and one save.

Ron showed me a fine fast ball. His breaking ball was not as consistent as he would like it, but he pitched well in winter ball and came up with a very good fork ball. Ron knew the

19

Blue Jay staff was blessed with an abundance of good arms and that is why he opted for additional work during the winter months. He wanted to sharpen his skills. The competition Ron faced really brought out the best in this quiet competitor.

One particular game Ron pitched in Minnesota shortly after he joined the club made a good impression on Coxie. With two outs and Kent Hrbeck at the plate, Coxie came out to make a pitching change. He had Jimmy Key throwing in the bull pen. Muss was throwing well, but Coxie said, "I've got Key ready." Muss never let Coxie finish what was on his mind. Muss said, "I can get this guy; I can get that fast ball in his kitchen." Bobby said, "All right, he's all yours." One pitch and one broken bat later, Ron was out of the inning. He showed that same determination in camp.

BRYAN CLARK, left-handed pitcher, 28 years old, 6 ft, 2 in., 200 lbs. Brian was obtained from the Seattle Mariners in exchange for outfielder Barry Bonnell on December 9, 1983. At the time, we felt he would be the left-handed short man we could use out of the bull pen. I always liked Bryan's stuff. I saw him pitch for the Seattle Mariners, from 1981 through 1983, and felt his acquisition would give us a good, strong left arm in the bull pen. He has a live fast ball and a snapping slider, but struggled with his control in the spring of 1984 and was sent to the minor leagues. Bryan started the season in Syracuse and after six starts, he was recalled to Toronto on May 13. He only appeared in 20 games the rest of the way, compiling a 1-2 record with a 5.91 ERA. Bryan struggled with his control most of the season, and we didn't have an awful lot of opportunities to use him. I feel if he can get command of his control and utilize the great arm he possesses, he could be a successful major league pitcher. Managers and coaches hate to overlook a guy with Bryan's arm, but he needed much better command of his stuff to break camp and go north with the Blue Jays.

STAN CLARKE, 24 years old, 6 ft, 1 in., 180 lbs, left-handed pitcher. Stan signed as a free agent in the amateur draft of June 1981. Clarkie had a cup of coffee with us in Toronto in 1983, making his major league debut June 7 in Oakland. He pitched in ten games, earning a 1-1 record with a 3.27 ERA. His first loss probably made the biggest impression on the young left-hander. He came into a game with a two-run lead in the ninth inning and gave up a game-winning, three-run homer to Reggie Jackson in a 7-6 loss. After the game, Stan sat for several minutes by himself and then went to the clubhouse with his head buried in his hands. Had he been a little more experienced, and possibly a little bit older, he might have realized that giving up a home run to Reggie Jackson to lose a ball game was not the end of the world. Several more accomplished pitchers ahead of him have done just the same thing. Reggie has well over 500 career home runs, and I'm sure he'll continue to hit home runs to win ball games against other very fine major league pitchers.

Stan was simply overpowering in the spring of 1984, early in spring exhibition games. He had a great fast ball and practically an unhittable breaking pitch. It looked as if he would be the short left-hander on the ball team. Overconfidence and inexperience caught up with him as the month of March came to an end, and opposing batters tuned up for the season. Stan suddenly experienced wildness and pitched ineffectively in Vancouver during a series with the Milwaukee Brewers. Bobby Cox made a switch after that series and recalled Jimmy Key from Florida; and Stan was headed for Syracuse. Later that summer, Stan hurt his arm and only made 29 appearances the rest of the year.

In 1985, Stan came off an arm injury, and started in the minor leagues to regain his solid pitching form. He certainly has a lot of promise and may eventually benefit from the early setbacks.

ROY LEE JACKSON, 30 years old, 6 ft, 2 in., 205 lbs, right-handed reliever. Roy Lee was obtained from the Mets on December 12, 1980 in a trade for utility player Bob Bailor. In 1984, Roy Lee started like a house afire. He was 6-1 at the All-Star break, but the second half of the season wasn't very kind to Roy. He finished up the second half 1-7 with a 5.24 ERA. Overall, with a 7-8 record and with a 3.56 ERA to go with 10 saves, Roy Lee had a pretty fair year.

Roy has an outstanding fast ball, that at times is overpowering, and a good slider. He is a power pitcher who battled a numbers game in spring training to make the club. He was unable to regain the form he showed in the first half of 1984. Roy Lee has compiled a 24-21 record with 30 saves

photograph by Dan Hamilton

Tom Henke

22

since becoming an American Leaguer with the Blue Jays, and he was one of the solid individuals on the ball club because of his leadership.

MATT WILLIAMS, 25 years old, 6 ft, 1 in., 200 lbs, right-handed pitcher. Matt was a first-round draft choice in June 1981 from Rice University in Texas. Matt pitched a little with us in 1983, as he was purchased from the Syracuse Chiefs of the International League on August 1, and started on the 2nd against the New York Yankees in Toronto. He won that game 13-6, pitching six innings. Five days later, Matt was not to fare so well. The Yankees knocked him out after only 17 pitches in the first inning. That is where his major league record stands — at 1-1, both decisions coming against the New York Yankees.

Matt knew he had little chance to make the club out of spring training, but felt that if he could have a couple of good outings and make an impression, his name might come to mind if someone went down to Toronto. Matt was a good trade prospect and he would go to a team not so well stocked with quality pitchers. He has pretty good stuff including a fast ball, a slider and a change-up, and he came off a fair year at Syracuse. Spring training exposure didn't do anything but help Matt Williams.

JOHN CERUTTI, 24 years old, 6 ft, 2 in., 195 lbs, left-handed pitcher. John was a second-round draft choice in June 1981. He's a promising young left-hander with a fair fast ball. He needs to develop more physical strength which will give him more speed. John has shown a really good curve ball, as well as a change-up which could be much better with a little more consistency and competence.

TOM FILER is a 18-year-old right-hander, 6 ft, 1 in., 198 lbs. He's a free agent signed to a Triple-A contract and was invited to camp as a non-roster pitcher. Tom came off an outstanding winter league season, where he posted 5 shut-outs. The winter league schedule is only 60 games; 5 shut-outs during a 60-game schedule is a great accomplishment. I really didn't know much about Tom other than that he pitched eight games for the Chicago Cubs in 1982. Tom went to Syracuse at the end of spring training.

TOM HENKE, 27-year-old right-hander, 6 ft, 5 in., 215 lbs. Tom is the compensation-pool draftee we acquired January 24, 1985 from the Texas Rangers, for losing Cliff Johnson as a free agent. He spent part of three seasons with the Texas Rangers in (1982-84). Tom has a good strike-out per inning ratio, and his ability and confidence stand out immediately. Al Widmar had to make some adjustments in Tom's pitching style to give him more control; but it is pretty obvious the man has a lot of ability. And he is a good learner. Tom is tall, and he's all arms and legs; if he's not in good mechanical rhythm, his ball could be anywhere, all over the place.

Al Widmar can move pitchers into good fundamental deliveries quicker than anyone I've ever seen. He took Henke out every morning and worked him hard, pantomiming pitching, just going through the motions without the ball, trying to establish a good, comfortable delivery. As he progressed, Henke started turning people's heads. We hadn't expected that of him. We hadn't known a lot about Henke other than the fact that the Texas Rangers, who did not have a particularly outstanding pitching staff, had not thought enough of him to protect him. They were wrong.

Henke got better and better as spring training went along. I knew it was going to be a tough decision for Bobby Cox. Henke had the ability to pitch on our team right away. We had Acker, Jackson, Musselman, Filer and Henke — all fighting for that last open position. I knew that if Henke did not make the cut, if he was sent down to Syracuse, Coxie had a great deal of confidence in the rest of the pitching staff.

Ball players are divided into two groups in spring training: one group hits on one field, another group hits on another field. This division saves a lot of time. Garth Iorg came into the locker room after the first day he batted off Henke and asked me, "Have you seen Henke throw yet? My Gosh, I didn't even foul off a pitch when I faced him." "I didn't hit a pitch either," I responded. "He throws good, hard fast balls; he's a little bit side-arm, and very tough to pick up. That guy is going to help us." Iorg is a big Tom Henke fan, as we all are. When Tom was sent to Syracuse, his ability was reflected in the winning of the Triple-A Championship.

CHAPTER 3

The Blue Jay Players

The Blue Jay Roster for Opening Day, April 8, 1985, read as follows:

Pitchers:

Jim Acker, Doyle Alexander, Bill Caudill, Jim Clancy, Jimmy Key, Dennis Lamp, Gary Lavelle, Luis Leal, Ron Musselman, and Dave Stieb.

Catchers:

Buck Martinez, Ernie Whitt.

Infielders:

Willie Aikens, Tony Fernandex, Damaso Garcia, Garth Iorg, Manny Lee, Len Matusek, Rance Mulliniks, and Willie Upshaw.

Outfielders:

Jesse Barfield, George Bell, Jeff Burroughs, Lloyd Moseby, Ron Shepherd, Lou Thornton, and Mitch Webster.

• • • •

WILLIE UPSHAW was at first base. There was no doubt he had arrived as a regular starter in the American league. The Blue Jays obtained Willie from the New York Yankees in December 1977 via the Triple A draft. Willie's early career with the Blue Jays was up and down; he was not a consistent player. In 1982, however, Willie was given the regular first

Willie Upshaw

26

base slot. He responded with 21 home runs and 71 RBIs, and the promise of greater run-producing potential to come. Willie's fielding has improved year by year as he works hard in his defensive skills during spring training, and before every game during the season. Willie is a dedicated player, and he is committed to improving his game. Willie is not a big man, physically, but he does have a lot of power. He was the first Blue Jay player to have 100 RBIs in one season (1983 with 104). He has developed into a quiet, consistant player who does his job well day in and day out. Willie Upshaw is one of the leaders of our team. We feel first base is well covered with Willie in the game.

DAMASO GARCIA was at second base. Damo has been with the Blue Jays for six years; he, too, was obtained from the New York Yankees. Damo was named to the 1984 All Star Team, gaining recognition as one of the finest second basemen in the league. He is a steady, reliable influence in the field, and is developing regularly as a solid line drive hitter. Damo combines his hitting with good speed, and is always looking for the chance to steal a base when he's aboard at first. Damo has been criticized by the media for not taking enough walks, (his greatest number of walks per season was 24) and it is true that the lead off man should take good advantage of the walk. Damo is a free swinger and a bad-ball hitter. He can hit balls up in the strike zone, or just off the dirt, and he hits them with authority. Damo is a real key to the Blue Jays's offense. He initiates a great many rallies for our team.

TONY FERNANDEZ was the shortstop. Tony looked forward to being the regular Blue Jay shortstop all through the year, after Alfredo Griffin was traded. Tony has great range and an uncanny ability to throw almost sidearm to first base, with great accuracy. He can switch hit from either side of the plate. Tony had a .270 average in 1984 over 88 games, and showed developing promise at the plate. He is a very real offensive threat to opposing hitters. Tony has great instincts, a rarity in a player as young as he is (22). He knows when and how to take the extra base; he knows game situations, and he is always heads-up on the field.

Third base was a platoon situation with RANCE MULLINIKS (hitting left handed) and GARTH IORG (a right-handed hitter).

Damaso Garcia

Rance was acquired from the Kansas City Royals in March 1982. He is probably one of the most consistent hitters on our ball club. Rance spent two seasons in Kansas City and, although he didn't play much, they were important to his development as a hitter and a solid major-league player. Rance made a point of listening and watching the Royals' hitters, George Brett and Hal McRae and Amos Otis. He knew that McRae had an uncanny knack for driving the balls to the opposite field, and he talked a lot with McRae about the selection of pitches and his thoughts at the plate: Hal knew, every time he went to the plate, what he wanted to accomplish and how he was going to do it. McRae spoke of his confidence in himself as a hitter and his ability to stay within himself at the plate; he did not try to pull every pitch. McRae stressed the importance of pitch selection, saying it was vital to pick a particular pitch and to stay with it. Rance made a mental note of this, and his hitting style reflects the advice. Rance Mulliniks expects a lot from himself and he works hard to make sure his swing is solid. He likes the ball away from him, over the plate, and he will wait patiently for his pitch. Originally signed as a shortstop by the California Angels, Rance has now become a solid third baseman and an integral part of the team concept of the Blue Jays.

GARTH IORG is the third member of the original Blue Jays' team, also drafted from the Yankees in the expansion draft of 1976. Garth is a perfect example of the player who wasn't blessed with outstanding physical ability, but who has developed into a solid major league player through determination, confidence and good work habits. Garth is a valuable asset to the club, not only because he platoons at third, but also because he can play second base, spelling Garcia, and he can fill in at shortstop should Fernandez go down with an injury. Iorg has also worked behind the plate in spring training, as an emergency catcher.

Rance Mulliniks and Garth Iorg are very similar. They're both slightly built; and they are both intense players with unusual names. We call them *Mullinorg*, putting their names together to make one player. Both men are spray hitters, hitting to all fields. Neither one is a power hitter. Each is talented defensively in the field, and they are both knowledgeable players. Their relationship with each other is

photograph by Neal Sadja

Tony Fernandez

30

solid. Each will ask the other for advice: "Where are you playing Don Mattingly, off the line or in shallow?" "How about Ricky Henderson? Let's crowd him up close, real tight." They talk a lot. When Rance starts a game, he always goes over to Garth, "Hey, Iorg, get your bat. We're going to run this right-hander out of here. You're going to be batting for me next time." There is no competition. Each man plays as hard as he knows how to play to win. Each man knows that he is a very valuable member of the Blue Jays' team.

JESSE BARFIELD was the rightfielder. 1985 was a big test for Jesse Barfield. We had traded away Dave Collins to give Jesse an opportunity to play every day (previously, Jesse had platooned with Collins in the outfield). Jesse had become very patient at the plate. He had learned to be selective and to wait on pitches that he could drive and hit. We all know what awesome strength he has. He doesn't need to swing hard, his arms and shoulders are very powerful from a daily regimen of weight training and working out. Jesse gets more consistent at the plate as he gains more confidence, day in and day out. He no longer fears being taken out of the line-up after an 0-for-4 at the plate; he knows he's going to be the regular rightfielder and he can relax at the plate. Confidence builds ability. Jesse gave us power, RBIs and solid defense.

Jesse Barfield has an outstanding arm. He ranks as one of the better throwers in the American League. He has good velocity and a lot of carry; he can throw the ball a long way, and accurately. The key to throwing from the outfield, as from behind the plate or from the infield, is getting rid of the ball quickly.

A lot of outfielders take a long time to wind up, throw and let go of the ball; they must get in proper position to throw, and it all takes time. While an outfielder is setting himself up to throw, the runner is running toward the base, getting closer and closer. Although the fielder might have a very strong arm, his inability to get rid of the ball quickly, with an accurate throw, makes him worthless to a team because the arm strength itself is not enough.

Jesse works very hard, and he has both quickness and strength. During batting practice, Jimy Williams would take all his outfielders to the outfield and hit balls up against the right-field fence. They practised their throwing positions: they took one-hop line drives and practised the timing of

31

Rance Mulliniks

throws and delivers (although practice is three-quarter speed, the motion is the same). Infield practice is crucial. Fielders must get in the *habit* of throwing, and Jesse does that very well. He throws a lot, trying to hit the cut-off man, trying to keep a low trajectory throw that the infielders can handle (thus cutting off the ball if necessary — when a throw is off line, they can relay it).

Jesse's aggressiveness, his ability to charge the ball, the strength of his arm, and the quickness with which he releases the ball, all mean that runners don't run on him any more. Third-base coaches are well aware that you can't go from first to third on Jesse Barfield. If the ball is hit near him, and he doesn't have to run 15 or 20 feet to either side, you can't *even* take an extra base on Jesse Barfield. He has become that accurate! He has a lot of pride in his work, and he practises day in and day out. Jesse is both an offensive and a defensive player for us. He can change the game.

Jesse's speed as a runner is very deceiving, and most people don't realize how fast he really is. He's a big man — weighs probably 215 — but he has outstanding speed. He is rarely thrown out for stealing. Jesse runs in crucial situations, so his steals add up to big stolen bases. He is not the type of runner who takes off and runs at whim: he watches the signs, and occasionally, he gets the green light, where he can pick his pitch and run at will.

Jesse Barfield is always learning more and more about the game. One thing that we all forget is the fact that Moseby, Barfield and Bell are each only 25 years old. They're just now becoming complete, polished players; they are still learning the intricacies of the game: where to take the short cut, how to steal bases, how to cut off balls in the outfield. They're just learning the game the major-league way.

Jesse is a very sincere person, with a lot of respect for his wife and a lot of respect for his family. I feel that he is a very honest person. He goes out and gives an honest effort every day. He takes a lot of pride in having his family with him; sometimes that's difficult for a young man in a game where the macho image is so often projected. Jesse is very satisfied as a father and husband, and he's proud of it, *very* proud of it. He has a Christian, or religious, foundation that he's proud to talk about, but he's hardly a Bible-thumper. Jesse does not go around admonishing people for swearing, or drinking a beer

photograph by Suzanne Rayson

Garth Iorg

or chewing tobacco; but he has his beliefs and they're very strong. I respect him for it.

Young people in this game have a tendency to be influenced by people around them, and Jesse hasn't let that happen to him. This goes back, I think, to his friendship with Roy Lee Jackson, who was a rock for many of these young players. Roy Lee was very, very firm in his religious beliefs — maybe a little bit over zealous about it sometimes. His influence on both Tony Fernandez and Jesse Barfield was very, very important, and I think they both gained immensely by it. Jesse Barfield and his wife, Marla, are two fine individuals, and I think they have set themselves goals in their lives and are working hard towards accomplishing those goals. They have their feet firmly on the ground.

GEORGE BELL was in left field. George is from the Dominican Republic and he capitalized on his first opportunity to play every day in 1984, when he left spring training in Florida as hot as anyone, carrying his streak right on through the season with a fine .292 average, 27 home runs and 87 RBIs. He set club records for doubles (39) and extra base hits (69), and was named the Labatt's Blue MVP (an honour which is assessed after every game and compiled at the end of the year). After playing both in left field and right field, George moved into sole possession of left field in 1985. Bell's offence is somewhat overshadowed by his work as an outfielder. His hitting has improved immensely as a result of his good work habits and the coaching of Cito Gaston, the batting coach. He has also become a very aggressive outfielder with a strong throwing arm. Many baseball people compare Bell to his countryman, Pedro Guerrero, of the Los Angeles Dodgers. George is the type of player who can carry a ball club, and as he gained more confidence in himself, '85 would be a repeat of '84. George, like Lloyd Moseby and Jesse Barfield, is only 25, so the Blue Jays' outfield future looks bright for many years to come.

ERNIE WHITT was the left-handed hitting catcher platooning with me. Ernie has been with the Blue Jays for seven seasons. He was originally signed by the Red Sox in 1972, and was selected in the expansion draft on November 5, 1976. Ernie has become a very good run producer, with a lot of confidence at the plate. He had 15 home runs in 1984 with 45 RBIs.

Jesse Barfield

LLOYD MOSEBY was in centre field. Lloyd, a product of the Blue Jays' farm system has both great ability and great buoyancy. He is a team leader, and has great speed, coupled with a strong throwing arm. He had tremendous confidence in himself, and he carries that out to the field. He is a colourful player who may well be headed towards superstardom. Lloyd had 71 RBIs in 1984. The only real apparent weakness Lloyd Moseby has is the fact that he can't carry a tune, although he thinks he is a great singer. We have ample evidence to the contrary, however, every game, as we all listen to Lloyd struggle through the national anthems.

WILLIE AIKENS was the left-handed designated hitter, and a backup first baseman for Willie Upshaw. Aikens came from Kansas City in a trade for Jorge Orta. He hit 57 home runs and 197 RBIs over three seasons in Kansas City, and needed to regain his stroke in order to become a valuable asset for the Blue Jays. Willie certainly has an abundance of strength and power.

JEFF BURROUGHS was the right-handed designated hitter, purchased from Oakland in 1984 as a replacement for Cliff Johnson. Jeff, too, needed to regain his former stroke to become effective. He was the first player selected in the 1979 free agent draft by the Washington Senators, and was the American League's most valuable player in 1974, with 25 home runs and 118 RBIs.

RONNIE SHEPHERD, a right-handed hitting outfielder, is a good young player (24), who has not really found his grove yet. Ronnie has great, unharnessed power. He had a fine year in 1984 winter ball, with 9 home runs. He has great speed in the outfield, and can cover a lot of ground.

MITCH WEBSTER, a switch-hitting outfielder, was drafted from the Los Angeles Dodgers in 1979. He has been a good help to Toronto in the past, and has had a successful season in Syracuse in 1984, where he hit .300. He is not a power hitter, but does hit line drives. His hard-driving playing style endears him to a lot of players. Mitch always gives a good effort. He is speedy, and plays hard. He would be used as a pinch-hitter, and as a back-up player.

RICK LEACH, a first baseman, outfielder, and left-handed hitter, made the ball club as an extra fielder and possible defensive replacement for Willie Upshaw at first base. Ricky came to camp in 1985 as a Triple A player, although he did

37

photograph by Neal Sadja

Ernie Whitt and Rick Leach

38

play with the team in 1984. He has a pretty good bat, and a very good glove at first base. He plays hard, and plays to win.

LOU THORNTON, an outfielder drafted from the New York Mets organization, was somewhat of an unknown. Lou had played in the minor leagues for four years, although never higher than A ball. He batted 275 in Lynchburg with 67 RBIs in 1984, and at 22 was just beginning his baseball career, in the major leagues.

MANNY LEE, a shortstop, was drafted from the Houston organization. Manny is also from San Pedro de Macoris in the Dominican Republic, home of Alfredo Griffin, Tony Fernandez, and Julio Franco of the Cleveland Indians. Manny had played in Columbia, South Carolina, where he hit .329 in 1984, with 33 RBIs. He was 20 years old, a fine fielding shortstop, and good backup for Fernandez.

Blue Jays designated as Rookies Opening Day were Luis Aquino (right-handed pitcher), Kash Beauchamp (outfielder), John Cerutti (left-handed pitcher), Stan Clarke (left-handed pitcher), Kelly Gruber (infielder), Alexis Infante (infielder), Manny Lee, Fred Manrique (infielder), Fred McGriff (infielder), Colin McLaughlin (right-handed pitcher), Ron Musselman (right-handed pitcher), Mike Sharperson (infielder), Ron Shepherd, Louis Thornton, and Matt Williams (right-handed pitcher).

photograph by Suzanne Rayson

Epy Guerrero, Pat Gillick and Tony Kubek

CHAPTER 4

The Season Begins

FROM FLORIDA SPRING TRAINING, WE MOVED TO VANCOUVER for what I called a Practice Opening Day. We were going to play in a city that is a major-league city in every respect, except that it did not yet have a major league ball club.

We left Dunedin, Clearwater and Orlando, where we had played our spring training games, in what are basically minor-league ballparks, and travelled to the domed stadium at B.C. Place to play a three-game series against the Milwaukee Brewers. True, these were Exhibition Games. We all knew that. They were, however, more like regular-season games because of the big city atmosphere. Vancouver was a long way to go, but the trip was a festive one because we had escaped from Florida. Each player on the plane felt he had just about made the team, although we had not yet cut the roster down to the final 25 players (two or three guys were still in limbo).

Vancouver is a beautiful city, and we were to play Friday night, Saturday night and Sunday afternoon. We arrived late Thursday night and stayed at the Westin Bayshore, right on the harbour with fishing boats tied up behind the hotel. It was like a dream. We rented a car and drove around to Horseshoe Bay and on up into the mountains. A lot of players, particularly the Dominicans, had never seen mountains. Some had never seen snow before. We took the tram up to the Grouse Mountain Ski Area and marvelled at the contrast between the 70-degree heat in Vancouver and the snow and skiers at the top of Grouse.

Alas! we did not play very well in Vancouver. The Brewers beat us 6-3 on April 5, and 4-2 on April 6. We came back on Sunday April 7 to beat Milwaukee 4-3. We were thinking about the official Opening Day in Kansas City, and had a very laid-back feeling about playing Milwaukee. If we got a couple of hits, that was great. We really wanted to ease into the mechanics of playing on astroturf again for the first time of the season.

The lighting in Vancouver's dome stadium is not up to major league standards because the stadium has not made the adjustment for major league baseball. B.C. Place is a football stadium, and the lights need to be aligned in different directions for baseball. This has not yet been done because dramatic changes would be necessary to the present lighting system to gain the required mobility, and these are simply not cost-effective until the city has a major league baseball team.

The stadium itself has facilities very similar to those in the Hubert B Humphrey Metrodome in Minnesota. Again, the big changes, like adding the proper amount of dirt in the sliding areas around the base pads, and taking the concrete out of the floor of the bullpen (we walked about on temporary rubber matting), have not yet been made.

Vancouver was a relaxing time for us all, and I'm glad we were able to play there. We had the opportunity to ease into the new season without pressure, and the fact that British Columbians are very big Blue Jay supporters certainly sent us into the new 1985 season on a high note.

• • • •

Opening Day is in Kansas City, April 8, and it is always an exciting time. This one's doubly exciting for me because I'll be starting against the left-hander Buddy Black. Players come to the clubhouse early in the morning — everybody generally gets there early, and everyone has a new uniform. We've been through spring training in our spring-training uniforms, relics of the previous season. The brand-new 1985 uniforms give us a good feeling, because they are new and they're comfortable; they have a fresh new smell about them. We each

Opening Day at Exhibition Stadium April 16.
We lost to the Texas Rangers 9-4.

get a brand new hat, too. We're starting all over and everything is fresh. Everybody's excited. The club has new bats. . . . Everything starting the season is brand new. It's like a ritual. We open up the bat cases and look for a good bat to start the season. We try on our uniforms and make sure they fit properly. Moseby, Barfield and Bell, with their great bodies, stand in front of the mirrors, checking out their appearance in the new uniforms, making sure they look all right when they go out onto the field. People like myself, Gary Lavelle and Bill Caudill, we with the not-so-good bodies, try not to look in mirrors too much.

Kansas City is exciting. We have Dave Stieb going against Buddy Black. A lot of people felt that this opening day match-up would be repeated in the fall championship series. The Blue Jays were picked to win our division and Kansas City was picked to win their division. I lived in Kansas City and I was keen to play this opening day in front of my friends and in front of those fans for whom I had played for eight years. I was ready to win.

I had a pretty good spring training. I was feeling positive about what was going on with my batting and with my catching. I had thrown well, better than I had ever thrown in the past. We started the game and Black was as sharp as ever, and Stieb was as sharp as ever. I remember that I drove in the first run of the season with a sacrifice fly and thought "That's a great way to start. This is going to be a fabulous year for me."

The Blue Jays lost the opener 2-1, in what was indicative of the rest of the season's competition between the Blue Jays and the Royals: well-pitched games, low-scoring games and hard-fought contests every time we met. We could not generate any runs for Stieb this outing, and it was an indication of things to come for Dave in '85. Although Dave Stieb led the league in ERA, his won-lost record wasn't indicative of that kind of performance, because we just never really supported him with a lot of runs.

Two days later, after an off day, we faced Danny Jackson, another young Kansas City left-hander, and he beat us once again in another low-scoring game (1-0, decided in the tenth). The third game of the series was won by George Bell, who hit a tenth-inning home run off Quisenberry to win the game. Toronto 4; Kansas City 3.

Willie Wilson scores on George Brett's bases loaded triple, helping Kansas City beat the Blue Jays 7-6 on April 23.

Quisenberry generally has much more luck against right-handed batters than he does against left-handed batters. He is a low-ball pitcher with a sinker ball way down into the strike zone. Bell is a low-ball hitter and he got hold of one right in his wheelhouse, and hit it into the bullpen. That was a big win for us. We usually play well in Kansas City. I think the atmosphere of the ballpark, and the good club, help. This time, though, we lost 2 and won 1.

• • • •

The next series was away in Baltimore against the Orioles, April 12. Baltimore seemed to be one of the teams we would have to beat. We had Stieb, who gave us a 7-2 lead. We brought in Lavelle, who struggled. Gary had pitched well during the spring, and we knew that he was going to be a left-handed short man. He came in, walked a couple of batters, and Bobby Cox made the move to Caudill. Billy too had thrown well in the spring, with good velocity and good control. We were confident we were going to win the game, an important one, as games had always been tough for us with Baltimore.

The Orioles always seem able to come back. Baltimore scored six runs in the eighth inning, as Caudill gave up a three-run homer to Murray. We had sudden flashbacks of '83 and '84, and looked at one another, thinking "My God, I thought we got this problem fixed." Baltimore won the game 7-6. We were sure Billy Caudill would shrug off the loss and get back on track. As we know now, however, he struggled all year, like Dennis Lamp in 1984.

Billy was under a lot of pressure, much of it, I think, self-imposed. He'd come from a team that was middle of the pack, the Oakland As, and he had saved 36 games for them. If you transposed those numbers into our records of '84, putting 36 saves to our '84 record, obviously we would have won the Pennant. Thus, everyone thought winning with Billy Caudill would be a natural for us. No one wins easily. We learned that later on in the summer. When Billy Caudill, prompted, I think, by the media, came over to us, he said, "Don't worry about a thing, I'll win the Pennant for you guys and everything," along with a few other comments. He sounded really boastful. The media hyped Billy with questions like "Bill, how great are you going to be for the Blue Jays?" He'd play along with answers like "Well, I'm going to be real great. The fans can buy their playoff tickets. Don't worry about it, we've got it in the bag now." I think this kind of exposure came back to haunt Billy, and it was unnecessary pressure.

The fans showed their disappointment early. They had listened to all the hype and, when Billy had a couple of bad games early on, they booed him. I know that had to be the first time Billy had been booed; he was with a new team where he had just been introduced as a "Saviour", as the last piece of the puzzle made up to win the championship, and he was being booed. I think this was a big emotional setback for Billy Caudill, because he had always won before. He had always been successful.

Billy is a very sincere person. He works very hard, he has a lot of pride, and he was having a tough go. He was hurting, but he didn't tell anybody he was hurting — because he was "Cuffs", the levity man, the "Inspector" and he was tough. He was going to go out there and do it anyway. Sometimes it's

April 19 — Lloyd Moseby loses a close call at second base
to Cal Ripkin Jr. The Blue Jays squeaked by Baltimore 6-5.

easier to get the job done when you admit to yourself that you're hurting and things aren't going well. You might use some help, you might need to talk to somebody; you might have to come up with a new pitch. Pride is so strongly entrenched in baseball players' minds that we just don't want to admit a thing. "I can handle anything."

Immediately after Baltimore, we all moved to Toronto, and our first job after arriving was to find accommodation. This was difficult. There are not that many places available with six-month leases, and most Blue Jay players live in Toronto only for the course of the season. A lot of guys are anxious about where they're going to stay. Usually the players live in a hotel for a few days and look around the city. If they're lucky, they find a good house or apartment quickly. If not, life becomes expensive, as all players must pay for their own accommodations when in the team's home town. Unlike most teams, where the majority of players live in or near the team's hometown, only one Blue Jay, the batting coach, Cito Gaston, lives in Toronto. That's why people who have never been here before don't know what to expect. I have made arrangements to live down on the Lakeshore where I've always lived, and I'm really not that concerned about it.

Coming back to Toronto after Baltimore, everybody was high. We had beaten Baltimore 5-3 in the second game of the series, and we always like to get back to our home city for the first game of the year. It's a time of promise. Everybody talked about "promise" in spring training: this was our year; we were going to win everything now. When you get to your hometown and line up on the foul line for opening day, it's a great feeling. You have a lot of pride.

"Well, we made it through another spring. I'm here in front of my home fans again. Here in Exhibition Stadium."

A lot of things can — and do! — happen in Exhibition Stadium!

• • • •

The rookies are really hyper because they've never seen more than 400 or 500 people in the stands in the minor leagues, and now here's Toronto — a place they've never been before, and it's a full house. The air is cold and it's windy, but, all in all, the day is bright and sunny, and the fans are truly excited. They're happy to see the Blue Jays back; they too know that this could be a year of great things for the Jays, and they want to be a part of it. Most of them have supported the team phenomenally all year long, for many years — for the life history of the Blue Jays, starting from the first game in '77.

The big thing about our initial home series, was the fact that not only were the Blue Jays back in town for the opening of the '85 season, but Cliff Johnson was back in town as well, with his new team, the Texas Rangers, with whom he had signed on as a free agent over the winter. A lot of Blue Jay fans had objected to losing Cliff and were pretty vocal about it in their comments and letters to the newspapers. He had been a very popular player, and a very productive player as our DH; we hadn't really filled his shoes yet. Jeff Burroughs was our new DH and he had a pretty good spring. Should he regain his form, Jeff would be a very competent replacement. Still, Cliff was very popular. He was colourful; he was fun to watch on the field. He was a clutch hitter and could hit home runs — he had set a major-league record for most pinch-hit home runs ever by a major leaguer, all as a Blue Jay. So, when Cliff returned to Toronto, he got a very warm welcome, and although I know Cliff is a big macho guy and he wants to keep that tough-guy image, I think he was very touched, as Toronto fans were not at all shy about showing their respect for him when he came back to town.

Texas socked it to Toronto in the opener, 9-4. Mike Mason got the win and Louis Leal the loss. Toronto took the next two games, sending Texas home in a gloomy mood. Toronto then took two out of three from Baltimore, before losing two more to Kansas City. A mixed beginning at best.

It became apparent, however, as we moved further into our Canadian spring, that the Blue Jays were definitely going to make a run for it in 1985. Between the 24th of April and the first of May, we had seven wins in a row, and it put us in first place by half a game as of April 30th.

On May 1st, Jimmy Key became the first left-handed starter to win a game since October 4, 1980 — the first in 614 games. This was just unbelievable; it was an important milestone. We hadn't had anyone capable of winning a game from the left side until Jimmy Key emerged as a starter, and we knew Key was going to play an important role during the season. He had pitched well in relief in '84 and he came back as a starter in '85. We hoped Jimmy would be a solid fourth or fifth starter, giving us a good look, and really balancing out our pitching staff.

The win on May 1st (against California), our seventh in a row, tied the club record of seven consecutive wins, of which six came on the road.

California beat us on May 2nd, and the month of May turned out to be a miserable one for me. I was really struggling at the plate, with only four hits in April. I was going to go the entire month of May with only one hit in 30 at-bats, and a season total of 5-for-60 for the first two months. I felt the weight of the world was on my shoulders. I kept trying to adjust, trying to figure out why in the world I was doing so poorly, battling to get base hits. Looking back, I think I was really trying to do too much. I wasn't patient enough at the plate during my at-bats. I was not helping myself back in the dugout, either, as I sat browbeating myself everytime I made an out, thinking how I'd swung at a bad pitch, or had been over-anxious and not waited.

● ● ● ●

When you're in a slump, you spend an unbelievable amount of thinking on "Why am I in a slump? Why, all of a sudden, after a good spring training where I hit .270, hit the ball very well, drove the ball with authority. . . why can't I hit? I started the season in Kansas City and hit the ball hard a couple times in the first game against Black, and got a base hit off Jackson the second game I played. . . Why am I so over-anxious? I'm not waiting on pitches."

Earlier in 1982-3, Cito Gaston, our hitting instructor, had moved me up on the plate, made me look for the ball on the inside part of the plate and had me trying to hit it hard. This really worked well for me then: I hit ten home runs in '82 and '83, which was more than I had ever hit in the past (ten home runs in a platoon situation). During the first two months of '85, however, I was over-swinging. People made all kinds of suggestions from all different angles; I had fans sending me their last lucky dollar; and I had a couple send me a postcard that said, "Tough times never last: tough people do."

I hit balls hard, and they would be right at somebody; I'd hit pop-ups, and miss balls and swing at balls out of the strike zone. It was awful. George Bell came to me and suggested I try a different bat; Ernie Whitt said, "Don't worry about it.

photograph Canada Wide/The Toronto Sun/Norm Betts

Here I am in full battle regalia against Minnesota June 4.
Willie Upshaw, George Bell and I all hit home runs in this game
as the Blue Jays won 9-2.

50

You're not swinging that badly, you're just going through bad luck." Garth Iorg said the same thing, "I've never seen anything like this. You're really not swinging the bat that badly — you're just not getting any hits."

Well, I certainly knew I wasn't getting any hits. I remember a game in Toronto, against the Twins. The fans were chanting — not all the fans, mind you, but several fans were chanting: "Oh-72 . . . Oh-72. . . ." It was June 4th — and they weren't chanting about the temperature or anything else; they were chanting about my batting average because I was hitting .072. That night I got three hits off Frank Viola, including a home run. By June 4, I already had had a better month than I had in all of May.

● ● ● ●

Slumps start with a mechanical problem. Obviously you're not doing something properly: you're pulling your head off the ball a little bit; you're not waiting on the pitch long enough; you're not selective at the plate — you're swinging at bad pitches. . . . Something mechanical is causing the problem. As a slump develops and continues, it becomes mental. You begin to imagine that you're doing things wrong; you start to wonder if your foot's in the right place, or if your hand is in the proper position (should it be higher or lower?); you wonder if your bat is too heavy. Do you need a lighter bat? Is the handle too thick? Should you use pine tar or rosin? There are many, many things you try to change, and not just for superstition's sake.

A good batting stroke is very similar to a good golf stroke, at least that is the theory held by Charlie Lau, former batting instructor for the Kansas City Royals (He taught George Brett and Hal McRae, among others). Charlie always talked about weight transfer and shift, about hitting the ball with the back of one's hand, and having a solid, motionless follow through. This is a same technique a good golf pro will teach you. According to Charlie, any batter, be he right-handed or left-handed, uses his front hand, hits the ball with the back of that hand, and extends the swing through the strike zone. This enables him to stay on top of the ball, hitting with a downward swing which results in more carry, greater distance and more consistancy. The front or bottom-hand lead means that the batter's head should remain motionless throughout the follow through, avoiding a distortion in either the swing or the follow through.

Three of the toughest hitters in the American League — as far as trying to get them out — are George Brett, Don Mattingly and Wade Boggs. They all have good batting strokes and demonstrate a lot of patience and intense concentration, as well as good control, when they're at the plate.

George Brett does not move off the ball when he hits; he does not try to pull the ball in one direction all the time, but, instead stays with the pitch. A pitch outside will be hit to left field; a pitch down the centre will be hit towards centre field, and an inside pitch will be hit to right. George begins his batting practice every day by hitting the ball towards third base. He stays on the ball, driving it towards left field. As he adjusts his swings and gets more aggressive in practice, George moves the ball around to right field. Soon he is hitting only line drives to right field. He never over-swings. George is patient. He waits until the last possible moment to decide what pitch it is before committing himself. His ability to wait places him in the minority of baseball hitters.

Ted Williams, probably the most disciplined of all hitters, has said time after time that the single most difficult sports feat is the batsman's ability to hit a 90-mile-an-hour, round ball with a 35 inch piece of wood. Mickey Mantle sometimes made a decision to hit a certain pitch well before that pitch was even released. Other sluggers do the same thing. We all see this when players take big swings at the ball, and don't even come close to it. When Cliff Johnson swings, and his hat falls off, he has decided (prior to the release of the ball) what the pitch will be, and where it will be. Cliff is swinging away entirely on intuition.

Don Mattingly, who has a rather unorthodox hitting form — (he turns his front toe inwards towards the plate, and stands in a slight crouch) extends his swing, leading with the lower hand, right through the strike zone. Mattingly has intense concentration at the plate. He talks to himself constantly, maintaining a running commentary on the pitches and his reaction to them. Like Brett, Mattingly can move the ball around with the pitch, although his greatest strength is to right field. Don likes the ball down and over the plate; he is a great low ball hitter.

Wade Boggs, from Boston Red Sox, is another one of the

great hitters in the League. He, like Brett, utilizes the entire field, and is a very difficult man to pitch to. He does not have the power of a Brett or a Mattingly, but his consistency and ability to get two and three hits a game is remarkable. Like Brett, he waits on the ball and doesn't commit himself until he has judged its flight. Boggs' concentration level is also very intense. He is a very superstitious guy, and runs out onto the field everyday exactly at 7:17. Wade scratches a little symbol in the dirt before he steps into the batters' box, and he believes that symbol forms part of his concentration pattern.

Slumpers study films. Cito Gaston and I looked at films from '82 and '83. We finally detected something. It seemed that we had spent hours and hours pouring over these films; but both of us had overlooked one particular triggering mechanism which by its omission was causing me so much grief. I rock back and forth at bat, shifting the weight from my front foot to my back foot, back and forth, just kind of an easy rock. As the pitcher goes into his delivery, and drops his arm down to wind up and throw the ball, I cock myself by bringing my left foot back and setting; my hands cock at the same time. During my slump, I was not giving myself the chance to set; I was moving my left foot back, touching the ground, and going immediately forward, taking all of my weight forward and not allowing my hands to come through. I should have moved back, set in, cocked my hands, and *then* stepped forward, giving my body a chance to get the weight shifted back. Because I failed to set myself properly, my bat was extremely slow, causing me to miss a lot of pitches I felt I should have hit.

Once we had figured out that flaw in my approach, Cito and I were both very relieved, and as my set position got better and better, my swing got better and better. June was a good month for me as I hit .313, with a couple of home runs, and eight RBIs, in something like thirty at-bats. I was over the slump, and I was on my way.

The support that Bobby Cox gives his players is terrific. He could have come to me several times saying, "Buck, you're just not hitting them; I'm going to play Ernie." But he never did that. He remained with the platoon system, and he stayed with me. He had confidence in my ability as a catcher and felt that I would work out of my slump sooner or later. I thank him for his understanding and his faith.

CHAPTER 5

Toronto 2, Detroit 0 June 6, 1985

ON THURSDAY, JUNE 6, WE STARTED A STRING OF 27 STRAIGHT games with the Eastern Division. Many people had questioned our lead in the American League East because we hadn't played a lot of games against Eastern Division teams. As of the 6th we were 5 games ahead of the Baltimore Orioles with a record of 35-16. We started off with the World Champions, the Detroit Tigers. The Tigers were chasing us. They were in third place, 6½ games behind. Toronto fans were excited. Everybody in the city was waiting for the Tigers to come to town. "We'll show the Tigers" became a regular slogan and, naturally, there was also a lot of enthusiasm because Tiger fans too were coming to Toronto.

My wife, Arlene, drove me to the ball park and, as I got out of the car having kissed my seven-year-old son, Casey, goodbye, she said, "Hit a home run tonight." I chuckled. "Hit a home run! — I'm not even going to play. They don't have any left-handers. Hernandez is the only shot I've got late in the ball game. And you know if I do play, it'll be pinch-hitting, a pinch-hit home run is a little bit much to ask, isn't it . . . the way I've been struggling?" We both laughed, and she said, "Well, I just feel you're going to hit a home run today."

Key was pitching against Dan Petry. There were some 35,000 fans in attendance, and the stadium was electric with

54

anticipation. Jimmy Key came into the game throwing well. He'd done a really good job for us as a starter, as had Petry for Detroit. We knew we had a tough contest. Petry has really been overlooked a little bit by the media, because of Jack Morris being on the same team. In fact, Petry has done a solid job of starting for Detroit all along, and I think both pitchers are comparable; you can really put them in a shoe. They're both outstanding pitchers and they both do a great job.

All the Tiger fans were dressed in orange and black, displaying their Tiger hats very proudly. They were a colourful sight.

Jimmy Key took a no-hitter into the ninth inning. He had a perfect game until the sixth, when Tom Brookens reached on an error. It was a classic game — Petry and Key matched up in a pitching duel: ten solid innings from Petry — six hits, no runs; Jimmy Key — ten innings, two hits, no runs. Both teams had opportunities to score, but the pitchers really knuckled down. Detroit left eight runners on base, and we left seven.

Jimmy Key's hopes of a no-hitter vanished when Tom Brookens lined a solid single to left. Key, as he's done so often, shrugged it off matter-of-factly, and settled down to go after the win. This is an outstanding quality for a 24-year-old pitcher, "Now I gotta buckle down and win this game."

Key's no-hitter into the ninth inning reminded all of us of Jim Clancy's game in 1982 against the Minnesota Twins. Jim had pitched a perfect game through eight innings — not a single runner had reached base. This all ended for Clancy with the first batter in the ninth. Randy Bush got jammed on a pitch and broke his bat looping the ball over Damaso Garcia's head at second base. The hit itself was quickly erased in a double play and Clancy got the final out of the game. We went on to win that one as a one-hit shut-out for Clancy. The excitement as Clancy walked off the field, and in the last three or four innings, every time he walked to the mound, was electric. Fans would stand and cheer at their seats, applauding his efforts.

Just as Clancy's win went by the wayside, so did Jimmy Key's. A perfect game, a no-hitter, out the door. We were in the tenth inning. Key gave way to Gary Lavelle for the eleventh, and Lavelle retired him out of the inning, allowing one hit, one run. Acker came in. He gave up a hit and a walk, but still escaped the inning without any trouble, no runs

photograph Canada Wide/The Toronto Sun

Toronto fans called me out for an encore salute when I hit the
game-winning homerun against Detroit June 6.

across. Manny Lee pinch-ran for Ernie Whitt in the tenth inning; so I went in and played defence. Hernandez was coming in to pitch for the Tigers in the eleventh. I knew I'd get a shot at bat against Hernandez if the game continued to go scoreless. As luck would have it (and, by the way, things were not going too well for me at the time — I was batting .134), Hernandez hurt himself diving for a bunt off the bat of Lloyd Moseby. He finished the eleventh, but couldn't make the call for the twelfth. I was the third batter in the twelfth inning.

Sparky Anderson went to Aurelio Lopez who had struggled a bit in 1985. Lopez pitched well in 1984; he teamed up with Hernandez for the best bull pen in all of baseball. I hadn't had an opportunity to face too many right-handers, so I thought seriously about what I was going to do, and what I expected from Lopez. George Bell led off the inning and got hit by a pitch. First base, nobody out. Lenny Matuszek was the next batter, he let fly deep into left field, but not deep enough for Bell to tag up. One out and a runner on first base. I came up to face Lopez. I'd faced him several times before. I even caught him back in Kansas City years ago. I knew he had a good fast ball as evidenced by his nickname, Señor Smoke. He had also had a pretty good breaking pitch. I was looking for one thing only, though. I was looking for a fast ball. And I got one, the first pitch he threw me. A high fast ball and I fouled it straight back. I felt pretty good; I knew I had a chance to get on. The next pitch I saw really well, but it was outside, and evened the count at 1-and-1. Then once again Lopez came in with a fast ball and I fouled it back. I took a pretty good swing at it, but pulled my head off it a little bit. I looked down to third base coach — he was putting both hands on his face, indicating that I was pulling my head off the ball. (He always pats his cheeks and says, "Keep your face on it. Keep your face on it.")

Now I was in the hole, one ball and two strikes. I shortened on my stroke a little bit, thinking I just had to make contact and try to hit a line drive. I had to keep the ball off the ground, because if I hit it on the ground it was a sure double play and we would be out of the inning.

Lopez set and unloaded a pitch. I picked up the spin, and recognized it was going to be a breaking ball, but not a good breaking ball. It stayed out over the plate, and didn't break away from me. I swung and made good contact and felt the excitement as the ball jumped off my bat toward left field. I knew Bell had good speed and he could score if it was off the wall. I wasn't really looking, but I sensed, because of the excitement of the crowd, that this ball was going farther than I thought it might. Finally, as the roar went up around the stadium, I realized that the ball had sailed out of the ballpark. I had just hit a two-run home run in the twelfth inning to win a ball game against the Detroit Tigers. Wow!

I was ecstatic. I didn't know whether to jump up or whoop and holler, but as I trotted toward home plate behind George Bell, I was very, very satisfied, very pleased. All the players rushed out to the field to congratulate me; we had won the game. Jim Acker got the win. I remember thinking "Arlene told me to hit a home run today."

Later, when I got home Arlene told me that as soon as I was put into the game, she set Casey down in the bedroom and made him listen to the radio, while she started running the shower in the bathroom. She wasn't taking a shower; she was just trying not to listen to the ball game because she feels she's bad luck for me. She kept hollering through the door at Casey, "Tell me when he's coming up." Casey was excited. He's old enough to realize what was going on with the Tigers and the Blue Jays, and the great rivalry they have.

"Is he up yet? Is he up yet?" Casey hollered back, "Yeah, Mom, he's up now." When I hit the home run, Casey wouldn't believe it. He was astonished. It wasn't the fact that I hit a home run, but the fact his mother knew I was going to hit a home run. He raced into the bathroom, "Mom, Mom! He hit a home run, he hit a home run!" Then he sat down on the floor and looked at her and shook his head and said, "How did you know?", and he started getting tears in his eyes — "How did you know?", and he started to laugh.

CHAPTER 6

Mid-Season Pain and Triumphs

ON JUNE 13 WE WENT TO BOSTON TO PLAY THE RED SOX IN A four-game series. We were still in first place, five-and-a-half games ahead, but we knew Boston had an explosive team and we had to try to nullify them somewhat. We had a 6-2 lead in the first game, which we eventually lost in a four-run seventh inning: Boston 8, Blue Jays 7.

This was a really tough loss to start the series, especially in Fenway. Fenway Park has a way of jumping up and biting you — there's nothing like it because fly balls suddenly turn into doubles; line drive home runs in other parks are singles off the wall (played very well by Jimmy Rice in left field); and visiting hitters always have a tendency to over-swing because the green monster is staring you in the face, only 315 feet away, down the left field line.

Naturally, the Boston pitchers are well aware of hitters' weaknesses, and what hitters do when they come into Fenway. Actually, if you come in with the proper perspective, you don't change anything in your batting style. A ball hit up in the air and to the left has a chance of being off the wall, or into the net. But you can't make any adjustments trying to throw hits up there on that wall, because you'll get killed — pitchers will wear you out, pitching you away, and really take advantage of your trying to pull the ball on the wall.

In Game Number Two, Oil-Can Boyd, who was really hot the first half of the season, went all the way holding us to one run on eleven hits, for a 4-1 victory. Once again, we were unable to get some clutch hitting. That was two in a row in Boston.

Saturday, in Game Number Three, Gary Lavelle walked successive batters with the bases loaded, to give Boston three straight victories. It seemed as though we just could not do anything right in Fenway. Pudge has never had any trouble with walking people; but this time, he was never even close to the strike zone and walked two in a row with the bases loaded. The Fenway fans, of course, went berserk.

Boston had high expectations for the season because they are such a great offensive club. With Rice, Armas and Evans in the outfield, Bill Buckner at first, the great-hitting Wade Boggs at third, and Rich Gedman behind the plate, they have a line-up that is just unbelievable. We knew that they would be tough in Fenway, but the four-run eighth inning on Sunday was the last straw. We left Boston with our tails between our legs and a slim three-and-a-half lead — reduced from five-and-a-half. I don't think the club was down any more all season than they were after that series.

We had a chance to get back at Boston right away. After we took a short trip to Milwaukee for three games (where we won one out of three), Boston came to Toronto on the 20th of June. We knew we had to play them tough in this series, because Boston had all the confidence in the world — they were sky-high. One could feel the tension in the air. Both clubs were very competitive: Boston had a lot of ability on their team; we had a lot of ability on our team. In Game Number One, we were down at one point 5-1; but we came back with three runs in the seventh to beat them 6-5.

WE COULD BEAT THE RED SOX. They were human.

Saturday and Sunday we played very tough games: Saturday we beat them 7-2; Sunday they beat us 5-3 . . . after a rain delay of three hours and sixteen minutes.

I remember Sunday's game: Bobby Cox had Dave Stieb slated to pitch, but he got a weather report that said it was going to rain, and he didn't want to waste Stieb. He started Ronnie Musselman. We were leading 3-2 when the game was interrupted by the umpires because of the rain. The delay seemed interminable and the umpires were pretty uptight;

they didn't want to call the game and then have the sun come out. It was an official game; we had a chance to win if they did call it. But we waited and waited.

Finally, during one of the downpours, Garcia went outside to the dugout and blurted out, to no one in particular, "Why doesn't somebody make a decision?" Joe Brinkman, the crew chief, who was there, turned around and jumped right in his face. "I'm the umpire here; I'll make the decisions. Don't you say anything about what's going on here!"

Brinkman had caught everybody by surprise, because there was no reason for an argument. Bobby Cox was really upset; he got in between Garcia and Brinkman and just went hollering up one side and down the other. It was one of the darnedest arguments I have ever seen during a rain delay. Bobby eventually got thrown out of the game.

And we eventually lost the game. The Red Sox rallied with two in the eighth and one in the ninth inning, and beat us, after that interminable rain delay of three hours and sixteen minutes. We should have won the game. . . .

• • • •

Sunday, June 23rd, we were all in the dugout. Not much was going on. Bruce Kison was pitching for the Red Sox, and he was giving us a tough ball game.

Bruce is a tremendous competitor. He had started with the Pirates, moved to the Angels and is now with the Boston Red Sox, having signed on as a free agent. When Bruce gets on the mound, he becomes a totally different person; he will do anything he feels will help him win. Bruce regularly pitches inside to batters, tight inside; he can make some great pitches and really intimidate batters. Sometimes, however, the ball gets away from him, and he hits the batter, accidentally, and even sometimes, I'm sure, on purpose. This is all part of Bruce's pitching plan; he is not out to hurt anybody, but he is dedicated to winning games. That's all he was trying to do on Sunday — just win the game.

Kison's pitch came inside on George Bell, hitting him in the shoulder. Bell didn't hesitate. He broke directly towards the mound, where Kison stood with his arms down at his sides, almost like a challenge. Kison didn't raise his hands, didn't throw his glove off or anything; but George jumped up and gave him a karate kick, hitting Kison's hip. George's momentum carried him past the mound, and as he turned around, he

61

George Bell delivers a karate kick to Bruce Kison after
Kison hits him with a tight inside, wild pitch June 23.
Toronto beat Boston 8-1.

saw Rich Gedman, the Red Sox catcher, coming behind him. George promptly landed a one-two punch on Gedman's forehead — Bell was right on the money with the one-two. Then he glanced the other way and dodged away out to the third-base side of the mound.

The Blue Jays piled out onto the field. Acker grabbed Kison and took him to the ground. Bob Stanley and Mark Clear were out there trying to get at Bell; Bell ran over to Wade Boggs, and Boggs held up his hands, waving "Not me! Not me!" There was a tight mass of players, all fighting. John Sullivan had hold of Kison, and both of them were on the ground. Bill Buckner hollered at Sully, "Let him go! Let him go!" and then — I still can't believe this happened — Buckner kicked Sully in the face, with his shoe, twice. The Blue Jays went wild.

A fight is a fight; but we're all ballplayers, we're all basically in the same mould, and we just don't do anything like that. Buckner's action was ugly; it was really uncharacteristic of a baseball fight. Usually, we get into pushing and shoving matches, grabbing onto old friends and dancing around a little bit. Normally, there is not too much damage. But this fight was nasty.

When Kison and Acker got back on their feet, Kison asked, "What's your name?" He didn't recognize Jim, he had never seen him before; but he wanted to know who Jim was, in case they had a fight again.

Finally, we all got separated, and things calmed down. Kison went back to the mound. He wasn't thrown out of the game, although the umpires threw Bell out for charging the mound.

Ernie Whitt came up to the plate. Earlier in the game, Kison had thrown one over Ernie's head, knocking him off the plate. Now Ernie was up with the bases loaded. Ernie swung away and hit his first ever career grand slam off Kison. It was a magic moment. As the ball sailed over the right field fence, Ernie started about 30 feet down the line towards first base; and he was screaming at Kison, and he kept hollering at him all the way around the bases. We couldn't really hear what he was saying because the crowd was going berserk, but we knew it was something like "Take that . . . that's what you get for throwing at people's heads. . ." and so on, probably in somewhat less elegant language.

It was very gratifying revenge for all of us, and especially for Ernie, because he had originally come from the Boston Red Sox (they were his first team). It was a fitting end to a very emotional series.

• • • •

The June 20th Boston series is, I think, a good testimonial to Ernie Whitt and where he's come from in his career. When Ernie first came to Toronto, the manager and the general manager weren't real sure of his ability as a catcher. They felt he was a long way from being the quality catcher that they hoped he would be. As a left-handed batter, Ernie would have many, many opportunities to hit in a platoon situation. He certainly had catching ability, although he had been browbeaten often earlier in his career, on his pitch selection and on how he called a game; on his lack of self-confidence. I think managers misjudged Ernie. They didn't give him a whole lot to work with. What can you call when the pitcher can't pitch what you call?

I think Ernie took the criticism personally; he really didn't have anybody to sit down and work with him, to help him understand how to call a game. All catchers make mistakes — that's part of the game. But they need to call a game confidently. The catcher's confidence is passed on to the pitcher who must have faith in what the catcher calls; this in turn leads to a more-confident delivery from the pitcher, and everything gets better. A catcher who is hesitant about his call, and moves back and forth is wishy-washy, will have an adverse effect on the way the pitcher throws his pitch.

Ernie and I worked together: we sat down and talked about hitters and how to pitch to different hitters. We exchanged a lot of information. Ernie knew a lot more about the Toronto pitching staff than I did when I first came up; I had to rely on him a lot for information of what our pitchers were and were not capable of doing. Anyone can look at a pitcher and see what kind of stuff he has, but whether or not a pitcher can throw effectively in a pressure situation is something catchers have to learn.

I kept telling Ernie, "Have confidence in what you call. Your ability will take over. Be yourself, and don't worry about anything. If you do your homework and if you're prepared; if you know the weaknesses of those hitters coming to the plate on any particular night, make up your mind and call it according to those weaknesses. If the pitcher doesn't like the call, get time-out and go out to the mound and talk about it."

One fallacy that a lot of people have about the pitcher-catcher relationship is that the catcher calls every single pitch, and it's the catcher's fault if the batter gets a hit. Pitchers and catchers sit down together before practically every game they play, or at least before the first game of any new series. They discuss the hitters, one by one, and how they're going to pitch to them. There is no guesswork on the field. The catcher knows exactly what a Dave Stieb is going to throw to George Brett, or Hal McRae, or Lou Whittaker. What the catcher does is to make assessments during the course of a game as to how well Dave Stieb is throwing a particular pitch and whether or not he can get somebody out on a pitch that was discussed in pre-game analysis. The catcher must think on his feet during the course of the game and I think that's something that Ernie has continued to improve on, right on through the years.

Ernie Whitt was named to the All-Star team this year; he deserved to be. He has had a great year. Ernie was hitting very well at the All-Star Break, well over .300; he was hitting home runs, driving in runs and doing a great job.

Toronto fans have a soft spot in their hearts for Ernie Whitt because he was one of the original Blue Jays — "You had to love them . . . But they're so bad!" He is much more than that, though. Ernie Whitt is a good player on a good team; I think he will be around a long time.

● ● ● ●

On August 23, during the second game of a doubleheader against the White Sox in Cominsky Park, George Bell took a Dave Wehrmeister pitch and slammed it over the leftfield roof for a home run. This was but the beginning of what was going to be an awesome display of power over the next four days. The Blue Jays beat the White Sox both times on the 23rd, 6-3, and 10-6.

On August 24th, George took another pitch by Chicago's Tom Seaver (a 300 game winner) and hammered it into the centrefield bleachers, 455 feet away from home plate, for another home run. Bell became one of only 7 players in the history of baseball to have accomplished that feat. Chicago's centrefield bleachers are dead centre in the stadium, and are an amazing spot to hit a home run because most long balls usually get pulled to either left or right by right- and left-handed hitters. Dave Stieb picked up the win for Toronto, 6-3, and came within three outs of a no-hitter before Rudy Law and Bryan Little hit back to back home runs off him in the 9th. Lavelle came on in relief.

On August 25, against Floyd Bannister (one of the premier left-handers in the league), George Bell hit another home run over the leftfield roof. The Jays failed to catch Chicago, however, who had piled up a 4-run first inning against Jimmy Key. Final score Chicago 5, Toronto 3.

Moving to Minneapolis on August 26, Bell hit yet another home run off Burt Blyleven of the Minnesota Twins. It was George's fourth consecutive game with a home run, and the Blue Jays were right behind him with 11 more hits to beat Minnesota 4-3.

Bell is a ''streaky'' hitter, and his 1985 record reflects that fact. He hit .300 in April, slumping to .240 in May, and coming back to .300 in June. July was another slump, but in August his average jumped to .307 with 8 home runs and 23 RBIs. It seemed as if George was gathering steam for the Pennant showdown.

During August, Bell had an easy, fluid swing, and a motion that moved to hit the ball wherever it was pitched. He did not overpower that ball. This was his normal, smooth rhythmic batting style: George would lean back, sitting on his back leg, and throwing his shoulders back towards the catcher; he waited on the ball, and, as he hit it, his smooth bottom hand extended all the way through the swing — making him a very dangerous low ball hitter. George likes the ball from the middle of his thigh down, that's his strength. When he gets his act together, he drives hard line drives all over the park.

Subconsciously, however, after August, George developed a home run swing, and that hurt him. He started over-swinging, pulling off balls, feeling every time he swung, he would get a home run. George certainly had more than enough power to drive any ball out of the park, to any part of the field. What he forgot to do, after August, was to relax and go with the pitch.

George's swing was not his only problem. He was plagued with nagging injuries. The collision with Tony Fernandez in shallow leftfield at Exhibition Stadium left him with a sore back. In September, Bell developed a very bad cold, and he was sometimes unable to prevent his eyes from watering. His average fell to .239 in September and October. He hit one home run and had only 8 RBIs.

The September/October close of season was definitely a disappointment for George Bell, and for the team. George is an agitator, a needler. He gets on a ball club and teases everybody, keeping people loose. He has a great sense of humour. Early on in the season, when Moseby was struggling, George would mock Moseby's lack of production, saying, ''What's the matter with you, Moseby? You're supposed to be the leader here, and you're not hitting home runs. Come on! Show me that power!''

He has a lot of lighthearted banter; he doesn't want to hurt anybody, just to nudge people along.

George Bell's biggest problem is that he is a firebrand with the pitchers. Pitchers recognize that they can rattle George, and even though he is not intimidated by close pitches, he loses his composure when a ball comes tight inside. He points fingers at the pitcher, and rants and raves at him. This, obviously, breaks George's concentration, and every time a pitcher can do that, he has won a victory. George needs to understand that when he can maintain his cool, when he can hold onto his concentration, pitchers will not win by pitching him inside. Sure, they will keep pitching him tight, just to test him, needle him; but George will be a better hitter, a better player, if he lets those pitches go without incident.

George Bell has become an everyday player. His fielding in the outfield has improved dramatically within the last two to three years, as George has worked hard on his defense with Jimy Williams and Cito Gaston. Bell does not have the smooth graceful ability of a Moseby, or a Barfield, but he makes up for it with enthusiasm and desire. He has become a good throwing outfielder simply through practice and determination.

I think George learned a lot about himself during the pennant race. He went out and played everyday, despite his injuries; he never took himself out of the lineup. George was going to play, to try and help the team, and, as long as he was out there, he had a chance to help. I think George learned he had to become more consistent; he had to become consistent for six months, not just one.

George Bell has the ability to be a great player; for the first five months of the 1985 season, he *was* a great player.

CHAPTER 7

Out at Home

SEATTLE WAS THE MIDDLE OF A THREE-CITY, ELEVEN-GAME SWING in the schedule that kicked off in Oakland July 4 and would wrap up in Anaheim in a four-game series against the Angels.

The Fourth is always a special celebration, of course, but for this planeload of Americans, who worked north of the border, July 4, 1985 offered the added excitement of our being able to celebrate with our families in the United States, something we didn't get an opportunity to do very often. In my case it would be my first Fourth of July in the States in many years, and the fact that we were headed for Oakland meant that my mother and father and my brothers, Jim and Jerry, who all live just 70 miles away in Sacramento, would be able to join me, Arlene, and Casey for the event.

Holidays, of course, are working days for ballplayers. For the clubs, they are crucial attendance days, and elaborate promotions are invented and staged to fill the stands. Oakland was no different, and a huge fireworks display had been planned to light up the skies immediately following the game.

Our spirits were high. The Blue Jays' standing in the league, combined with the fact that several of the players had grabbed the opportunity to bring their families along, lent a holiday atmosphere to the road trip that I will never forget.

The opener against Oakland was a good one.

Tied 2-2 going into the ninth, we failed to score, and brought in our ace short man, Bill Caudill, to finish it out.

Billy walked the lead-off batter, catcher Mickey Tettleton, who the As then replaced at first base with pinch-runner Mike Heath. With nobody out, second baseman Donnie Hill sacrificed Heath to second, bringing former Blue Jay shortstop Alfredo Griffin to the plate.

On the first pitch, Griff lofted a little high fly ball into left field. George Bell appeared to be camped under it, but misplayed the ball for an error, sending Griff to first, while Heath moved on to third.

With runners now on first and third, the As sent yet another former Blue Jay, Dave Collins, to the plate; as Collins faced Caudill, you could feel the excitement.

There they were — the two principals in a trade initiated over the winter to strengthen the Blue Jay bull pen — each playing against his former team of just a year before; going head-to-head in a 2-2 tie, at the bottom of the ninth, with only one out, and the winning run on third.

In a situation like that, the only hope of blocking the run is to have the outfielders shallow enough to make an easy throw to home plate. And that's where they were — Barfield, Moseby and Bell, all in close. Caudill set. He took the sign from Ernie Whitt and delivered his fast ball.

With a line drive to centre field, just in front of Moseby, Davie Collins sent Mike Heath home, and the game was over.

Caudill, who had to have wanted the save badly, got tagged with the loss against his old club.

Collins got the game-winning RBI — what, for him, must have been the very private, special thrill of striking back at the team that traded him away after his finest year in the major leagues.

Oakland 3 — Blue Jays 2.

Not a great way to start a road trip, but we had the satisfaction of knowing we were still up one-and-a-half over Detroit, so we quickly put that night behind us and began to think about winning the next match.

After the game, the crowd was invited onto the field to enjoy the fireworks. As what looked like the entire 46,770 fans began to pour onto the field, I spotted Arlene and Casey making their way toward me. The stadium was filled with good, old-fashioned Fourth of July feeling.

It was quite a night.

Casey was excited. He was going to get a chance to sit in the dugout. I was excited, not only because it was the Fourth of July and I was celebrating it back in the good old U.S.A., after some years absence, but because I suddenly realized that this July 4th would be the first time the three of us — Arlene, Casey and I — had ever managed to celebrate it together.

The happiness of the giant throng was infectious. And because we were a part of it, watching what must have been the most spectacular fireworks display I have ever seen, we were a very happy family.

The Blue Jays came back on Friday night with an 8-2 win over Oakland; we lost on Saturday, and then bounced back again with an identical 8-2 score to take the final game, splitting the series 2-2. Then, on to Seattle, and the beginning of my end.

The Blue Jay-Mariner opener saw Dave Stieb and Jim Acker combine on a seven-hit shut-out: Stieb ran his record to 9 and 5, on five hits in seven innings, and Acker provided two strong innings of relief. The win, combined with the Tigers loss to Chicago put us two and a half games up.

Going into the second game against Seattle, Tuesday night July 9, I was a little concerned that I hadn't had much opportunity to catch Tom Filer who had just joined us that very day. I talked to Sully about what I should try to do, and we agreed that Tom wasn't an over-powering pitcher, that basically he was a controlled pitcher who had to utilize all of his pitches.

Tom has a sinker, a curve ball, a slider, and a change-up. We would simply have to make sure that he put them all to good use: that he threw strikes, stayed ahead of the count, and didn't walk himself into trouble.

Filer gave up a few hits in the first couple of innings but he was throwing pretty good stuff and keeping out of jams.

In the second, with Seattle third baseman Jim Presley on base and one out, Spike Owen — shortstop, hit a long fly ball deep into right. Jesse Barfield was there to make the catch and, as Presley started his run, he released a powerful throw that headed toward me in along the first-base side of home plate. I reached for the ball, caught it, then had to dive back

Here I am tagging Phil Bradley on his attempt to score in the
fourth inning of our game against the Seattle Mariners, July 9.
Bradley was out, and I was down for the count.

toward the plate to tag a headfirst, sliding Presley for the third out.

In the dugout between innings, everyone congratulated Barfield on that spectacular toss. I was sitting next to him and I said, "Jesse, it was great, but next time try to get it on the third-base side so I can get a really good shot at the runner."

Little did either of us know that that would come back to haunt me in the very next inning.

Gorman Thomas is an old friend from Milwaukee days. He had missed most the 1983 season following a shoulder operation. Now he was back in the line-up, facing Filer, as the designated hitter for the Mariners in this sixth game of our road trip through the West.

Gorman has incredible power. He is an exceptionally good fast-ball hitter with an impressive history of home runs. He uses a big bat, likes the ball out over the plate and has an uncanny sense of the strike zone for a big man. You have to try to pitch him inside.

You can never second guess these things; but with two strikes against him, with Phil Bradley on second, and only one away, I suddenly seemed to forget everything I ever knew about Gorman. I signalled Filer to try to sneak a fast ball by him, on the outside.

The rest, as people seem to like to say in books, is history.

Gorman drove the ball past Garcia at second base and into right field.

As Bradley started his run, I took my position at the plate and watched Barfield's throw to home drifting up the line toward the third-base side where I had asked him to put it. As I made contact with it, I could see Bradley out of the corner of my eye, and I knew that I was going to get hit. There just wasn't time to turn around.

As I tagged him out, Bradley caught me squarely in the left shoulder with a forearm, pummelling me to the ground.

Like everybody else in the Kingdome that night, I knew there was something seriously wrong with my leg. But I also knew that with my wobbly toss into left field, Gorman Thomas would be barrelling down the third-base line, so I forced myself into position to make that play.

I was still sitting on the ground.

Gorman, who also knew that I was hurt, seemed to be tip-

photograph UPI/Bettman Newsphotos

July 9 — Gorman Thomas of the Mariners tiptoes past me trying to score as I'm lying injured on home plate after being hit by Phil Bradley. I managed to tag Gorman out; it was my last play in 1985.

toeing, trying to get to the plate without stepping on me and causing further injury.

I tagged him out, held onto the ball and slumped in a heap.

"Well," I thought, "now I can take a break."

I didn't feel too good.

My teammates gathered around me quickly.

First-base coach Billy Smith came over; so did Kenny Carson, the team trainer, and Bobby Cox.

Bobby kept saying, "Don't worry. Don't worry, you'll be all right."

Jimy Williams said, "I don't know how you did it, Buck, but that was the greatest play I've ever seen."

I wasn't groggy. I had all my senses.

When they got me onto the stretcher, George Bell took an end of it and insisted on carrying his "Boockie", as he calls me, into the clubhouse.

"I'll carry him. I'll carry him," he was saying.

Gorman Thomas came to see me.

"Nice going, Martinez," he said with a big, nervous grin. "You got me booed! They booed me 'cause I didn't slide!"

I remember we laughed at that.

Then he asked me if I was okay.

"Yeah, Gor. I'm fine," I said, and thanked him for *not* sliding into home, or running right over me where I lay on the ground.

"Man, don't even talk like that," he said. "When Bradley crashed you, I could see you were hurt. I was just hoping I could find a way around you. I don't know how you did it, but you got me too."

An odd thing about this sport is that, despite all of the people you meet over the years, you don't strike up too many really close friendships. It probably has a lot to do with the fact that even your casual acquaintances are all too often traded away. Gorman Thomas is an exception, a true friend, and the fact that he came over to sit with me until the ambulance arrived, is proof of that.

At the hospital, I was rushed into emergency still wearing my uniform. My right leg was in a splint, wrapped in an air bag filled with ice. There was still no pain.

Examining my leg, after removing the splint, the doctor explained that with dislocations as serious as mine, the proper procedure was to apply pressure to the heel while pulling downward.

I remember trying to understand exactly what he was describing, when all of a sudden it became very, very clear. As the doctor pulled my foot downward, my leg bones popped back into the socket with a grinding, sickening crunch.

There was still no pain, but the sensation of those two large bones grinding against each other was almost more than I could bear. I lay back on the hospital cot and came very close to passing out.

I was given a room and told to make myself as comfortable as possible for the night. There was nothing more the doctors could do for me right away.

My ankle would need time to heal . . . a long time.

Later on, I called Arlene to tell her I was feeling fine. I told her I wouldn't be playing for a while, and that we should make plans to go home.

It was a bittersweet moment.

We had often dreamed about a summer in Kansas, a normal, relaxed summer like our neighbours, with nothing to do but barbecue, watch Casey play ball and hang out together. I used to joke that it would be nice to be able to wave to my neighbours in something other than a snowstorm. Well, there would be plenty of time for that now. I was going to be out of the line-up for awhile.

We hung up, promising each other that tomorrow would be a happy day.

But I was upset.

The Blue Jays had gotten off to such a great start . . . 1985 was our year.

We had the best record in baseball, and now this.

I think what bothered me most of all was that it was such a freak accident.

I had been hit harder, many times, by many different people.

In my first start in the major leagues, back in 1969 in Kansas City, Bob Allison, a 225-pounder former running back at the University of Kansas, had run over me at home plate. I'd been knocked unconscious, but I'd tagged him out. (I had also led off the next inning with a home run.)

Joe Lahoud of the Boston Red Sox had also knocked me out, and twisted my ankle in the process. Like Allison, he was also tagged out.

The only difference in my run-in with Phil Bradley was that my right foot had become stuck in the dirt around home plate.

In indoor stadiums, the dirt areas around the bases are often unusually sticky. This is caused by the humidity, and by the slow rate of evaporation. Baseball clubs don't seem to be able to prevent problems occurring in this area, and other players have also been hurt. Usually the cleats spring free of the clay, but on this particular day, my right foot stayed embedded in the ground. Then, when Phil Bradley and I collided, the weight of my body snapped the tibia and the fibula from my ankle bone. And that was that.

Alone in the hospital, I was somewhat relieved. I had been working hard all year, struggling hard to give the team everything I could, but I still wasn't performing as well as I should. It was hard to pinpoint, but in one sense my injury meant I could stop fighting with myself, for a while at least.

It should have been the last thing on my mind, but when I left the park there had been no score, and being a typical ballplayer, I was anxious about the outcome. I needn't have been, because Bobby Cox, Kenny Carson, Bobby Mattick and John Sullivan arrived at the hospital to see how I was and to fill me in on the details.

As it turned out, the game had gone four hours and thirty-three minutes when George Bell had finally scored a grand slam homer off Ed VandeBerg in the bottom of the 13th inning.

Ron Musselman had pitched the final three innings, giving up only one hit, and George's home run (his 17th, and his first grand slam off VandeBerg) had given Muss the win.

As they were leaving my hospital room, Bobby Mattick, my original manager in Toronto, told me that in all of his years in baseball, he had never seen a play like my last one at the plate. He then added that he doubted anyone would ever see another one like it.

That's when I told him that I, for one, hoped he was right.

The next day I flew to Sacramento to spend the night with my family before leaving the following morning for Kansas.

Arlene was a tremendous help to me, and although she shared my disappointment at being out of the game, she hid it very well.

Arlene knew, too, that this was the Blue Jays' year. Like me, she understood the excitement of a winning season, of taking part in a pennant race, of maybe going for the pennant itself.

"Don't you worry about a thing," she told me, "we'll just head on back to Kansas and go home."

"Home."

When Arlene says it, it's a million-syllable word.

Our family moves at least three times a year: first out of the home in Kansas, and into somebody else's apartment in Florida for spring training. Then, after six weeks, Arlene oversees the packing and the move to Toronto to set up housekeeping once again. After the season, it's back to Kansas.

"There are a lot of advantages to being married to a baseball player," she tells me, "but moving is definitely not one of them."

When we got to Kansas City, I made an appointment to see Dr. Paul Meyer who had been my team doctor when I was with the Royals. And it was on Friday of that week, after X-rays, we discovered that while the swelling in my ankle had reduced considerably, the bones had not gone back into place.

It was at this session, too, that I mentioned a pain in the upper part of my leg, near the knee.

Without even hesitating, Dr. Meyer said he guessed it was broken, and sure enough, it was.

I remember thinking at the time, "What else can possibly go wrong?"

As it turned out, the fracture near the knee was nothing that a simple cast wouldn't fix. The dislocation at the ankle, however, would require a screw to properly fix the bones in place.

One of my worries at the time was whether or not I would be able to handle my color-commentary role for TBS radio in Minnesota, something I'd done over the past three seasons.

I needn't have worried.

Screw in place, a cast on my leg, on crutches, and with

Arlene at my side for moral and physical support, I made it to Minneapolis where Arlene and I joined Tom Cheek and his wife for a quiet dinner, far removed from the pre-game hoopla and a lot of people I was not quite ready to see.

photograph by Dan Hamilton

Cliff Johnson was acquired from the Texas Rangers August 29.

photograph by Dan Hamilton

George Bell's second grand slam of the season August 2 against
the Texas Rangers scored Mulliniks, Garcia, and Moseby as
Toronto beat Texas 5-3.

CHAPTER 8

The Mighty Fallen

EVERYTHING WAS SET FOR THE NEW YORK-TORONTO SERIES IN New York — four games from September 12 through September 15. We hit New York $2^1/2$ games ahead after the Yankees lost a hotly disputed game in Milwaukee on a foul-ball call. We were psyched. The Yankees were psyched, and New York was going wild.

Thursday, September 12: Jerry Eisenberg of the *New York Post* called it "Baseball Thursday." The New York Mets took on the St. Louis Cardinals in Shea Stadium in the afternoon (and whipped them soundly 7-6, after watching a 6-0 lead evaporate), and across town, in the Bronx, Toronto and the Yankees faced off in a spirited night encounter. There were 53,000 people in Yankee Stadium for Thursday night's game, and everyone was wired. There is nothing like Yankee Stadium in a tight baseball race, because everybody in the stadium is a true baseball fan; they really know the game from its finer to its rougher points. Dave Stieb was on the mound for the Blue Jays against Ron Guidry: Stieb with the lowest ERA in the league; Guidry, the revitalized superman, with an 18-5 record for the season.

The evening started out well, as the Canadian national anthem and singer Robert Merrill were both given a long and very robust Bronx cheer. Cliff Johnson, the senior Blue Jay, went on record as saying, "That was the un-classiest thing I've ever seen in all my 38 years." I agreed. Stieb dominated the game until the seventh inning. Ernie Whitt hit a two-run homer off Guidry, and the Jays had a 4-1 lead. Stieb, who eventually walked seven in the game, struggled with his control at the start of the seventh inning. He walked Willie Randolph with one out and nobody on. Randolph batted eighth in the order. Bobby Meacham, the shortstop, followed with a ground ball up the middle — a natural double-play ball. Tony Fernandez fielded the ball all right, but hesitated before flipping it to Garcia. The ball hit Garcia in the back and rolled out of the infield. Error: Fernandez. The Yankee fans went crazy. Rickey Henderson, the lead-off batter, was at the plate. Stieb walked him on a 3-2 pitch to load the bases. That was Stieb's final walk, and he knew it as he slammed down the rosin bag in disgust. Bobby Cox came out to the mound for a pitching change. Gary Lavelle came in to face Ken Griffey, the left-fielder. Griffey hit a ground ball to third. Iorg threw to second, but Henderson, with his great speed, slid hard into Garcia, making Damo rush his throw to first. Griffey beat the throw. The Yankees had two outs. The batter was Don Mattingly. He hit a line drive through the hole at first base to make the score 4-3. Dennis Lamp came in to face Dave Winfield. Winfield hit a ground ball to the hole at short. Fernandez came up with it and backhanded it, but his throw to second was over Garcia's head. Mattingly was safe. Error Number Two. Henderson scored, tying the game. Ron Hassey was the batter. Runners at first and third. Two outs. Lamp got behind Hassey with two balls and a strike; the next pitch was a sinker ball. Dennis knew he had a base open and was trying not to give Hassey a good pitch. The ball strayed out a little too much over the plate; Hassey got hold of it and wafted it into the stands for his 12th home run of the season. The game burst wide open. The fans went berserk. The Yankee scoring machine was on the move.

The headlines in the newspapers the next day read "Jays fall when Fernandez fails," but Tony bounced right back. New York was not going to beat him or the Blue Jays for long.

• • • •

Game Number Two on Friday night had Phil Niekro, going for his 300th win, against Jim Clancy. We were all on edge wondering what the Yankee fans were going to do. Moseby came out of the dugout before the game, hollering, "Uh-uh, not me, they're not going to put my name in the books with Phil Niekro's 300th win." All of us wanted to see Niekro win his 300th game, but we did not want him to win it against us that night, although he was particularly sharp. Phil does well with his knuckle balls: he throws the soft one for control, and when he is two strikes up on a batter, he goes for the hard knuckler — which has a devastating break.

Just before the national anthems were played, Bob Shepherd, the Yankee's public-address announcer read out a statement: "We are reminded of a time, just a few short years ago, when our Canadian neighbours unselfishly risked the safety and security of their own embassy and countrymen in the Middle East and came to the aid of Americans held hostage, and provided shelter and safety, proving to the world that they are true allies and friends to America. It is traditional, therefore, that when a Canadian team comes to New York, we honour both Canada and the United States. Let us now show our respect for both nations during the singing of "O Canada" and "America the Beautiful." Good try, Bob. The fans applauded loudly. They appreciated the thought, but once again they had to boo the national anthem. Yankee fans were going to give support to the Yankees; that meant they were going to boo the Blue Jays regardless. I'll never quite understand the Yankee fans' thinking.

Al Oliver got two hits and drove in all three runs. Niekro only gave up 8 hits; he pitched nine innings in a valiant effort. During the eighth inning, I sat next to Cito Gaston. We looked out to the mound: Niekro was pressing his right hand to his side; his middle finger and his index finger had cramped up and were rigid against his palm. Phil was trying to pry those two fingers away from his palm so he could get his knuckle ball working again. Yankee trainer Gene Monahan and Billy Martin rushed out to see what the problem was; they started massaging Phil's fingers, trying to get the muscles to relax. Obviously fatigue had set in. Phil Niekro is 46 years old, and he deserved to be tired.

Clancy, Lavelle, and Henke really did outstanding jobs for us. Clancy pitched four and one third innings, and only gave up two runs. Lavelle came on to give three strong innings of

photograph Canada-Wide/The Toronto Sun/Fred Thornhill

Sometimes it's hard being a non-playing participant. Here I am during the series with New York at New York September 12-14.

two-hit baseball. He was followed by big Henke, who gave up one hit and had three strikeouts. Save Number 12. Just routine.

It was a good game for us, and it boosted our lead back up to two and one half games. We could win in Yankee Stadium: we could quiet the fans. Friday the 13th, we had beaten the Yankees in New York. The game was not real pretty. One play that might have indicated where the Yankees were headed, happened in the second inning after Hassey had singled, and Willie Randolph drew a two-out walk. Bobby Meacham jumped all over Clancy's fast ball, driving it to left-field where George Bell broke in on it. Bell misplayed the ball, and it fell over his head. Hassey scored easily from second. Willie Randolph, who had injured his hamstring in Milwaukee, was running from first, not at full speed. Third Base Coach, Gene Michaels, held him up as he rounded third, with no chance to score. Bell relayed the ball in. Bobby Meacham, sure he had a triple, barrelled into third, head down; he peeked around and looked up. Who should he see standing on the third base bag, but Willie Randolph? Uh-uh. Meacham pulled up stakes and raced back to second. Alas, no one was tagged out.

Our victory nullified the first game's results. The series was even at one apiece. Our mood was upbeat. We hadn't really hit Niekro that well: we had, however, played some good defence, made some good saves in the field, and basically played a good all around ball game.

Moseby was a good indication of the team confidence. On September 1, Lloyd made an announcement in the club-house: "Gentleman, don't worry about a thing. I'm going to take care of things from here on in." And take care of things is exactly what he did throughout the Yankees' series. Moseby provided a lot of offence, and made several key plays in the outfield. He was 7 for 17 in the series. His performance was a big personal boost for Lloyd, and for all of us.

Moseby is one of the kids who has risen rapidly through the Blue Jay organization. He signed early and was moved immediately to the major leagues. He struggled from his first appearance in Toronto in 1980: he was not ready. Lloyd was a young player out of high school; he had only played a couple of years in the minor leagues. Gillick's plan was to bring up a young player of Moseby's stature, put him out in centrefield, and let him learn how to play major league baseball in the major leagues. Lloyd undoubtedly suffered much anguish early on, hitting .229 in 19890, .233 in 1981, and .236 in 1982. Each year he gained more and more confidence. By 1983, he had a .315 average. Watching Moseby become a good everyday player, and watching Gillick stick with his young players, giving them confidence on the major league level, is what the Blue Jays are all about. Lloyd Moseby epitomizes Blue Jay player development.

Lloyd Moseby and Rickey Henderson grew up together in Oakland, California, and there has always been a friendly competition between them. They had played together and against each other in Oakland as youngsters, and now they play against each other in the major leagues. Rickey initially was with Oakland; now he is with New York. Both Lloyd and Rickey are very colourful players, and both are called "hot dogs" by other team players, because they always put on a bit of a show. Henderson has become one of the great players in baseball and he is showcased in New York. His ability as a lead-off hitter who can steal 100 bases and also hit 20 home runs, combined with his great centrefield defense, makes him a real asset to any team. Rickey is very much in tune with New York; he fits right in with the flamboyant style of that city. Even though he is from California, once he steps on the field, Rickey Henderson is all New York.

We call Lloyd Moseby and Rickey Henderson, *Little Rickey* and *Big Rickey*. When they get together, and Moseby is having a good series, he wants to put it on in front of Rickey. I think Rickey does the same. They are always kidding one another. When Niekro was pitching for his 300th win in Toronto, Saturday night, October 6 after we clinched the pennant, Moseby was sitting in the dugout. Henderson stepped into the batter's box, and dug his right foot into the dirt. Then he stepped out and looked over the field, as if to say, "What should I try to do now?" Moseby, who was relaxing, taking a day off and enjoying the pennant, hollered out at Henderson: "Get in the box, Henderson, you hot-dog!" Everybody on our bench broke up. How in the world he had the nerve to call any one a "hot-dog", I don't know. It was very funny.

Saturday night's game (September 14) pitted Jimmy Key against Bob Shirley, two left-handers. The Yankees got off to a fast start, leading 1-0 at the end of the first. We came back in the bottom of the second when Jesse Barfield waylaid a Bob Shirley sinkerball up the alley in right centre for a double. Garth Iorg followed with a double down the right field line, tying the game. The Yankees bounced right back to take a 2-1 lead.

Jesse Barfield came to bat again in the next inning, and jumped all over a Bob Shirley breaking ball, driving it deep into the leftfield seats, as fast as you ever want to see a home run leave Yankee Stadium. It was a rocket. (Jesse eventually hit 7 for 15 in the series.)

This key shot was indicative of Jesse's fine play all year. He hit .285 with 22 home runs and 80 RBIs, a great job. Jesse was especially consistent in August, September and October, day in and day out. Jesse reached base in 28 games straight at one point during this stretch.

The game broke open in the sixth inning when, with one out, and the score tied 2-2, Garth Iorg singled off Rich Bordi. Billy Martin went to the bullpen for ace reliever, left-hander Dave Righetti. I nudged Don Chevrier in the broadcast booth, "My God, this is a little bit early, isn't it?" It was a big gamble but I guess Martin was forced to take it. The Yankees did not want to lose two in a row in such a crucial series. Righetti has a good fast ball, and a great breaking slider. He also has a tendency to overthrow sometimes, and get wild. Our scouting report said we had to make him bring the ball down, because his fast ball is up in the strike zone.

Four balls in a row, and Ernie Whitt walked. The Yankee fans began to stir. Righetti fell behind Mulliniks with two balls and no strikes. Then he found the strike zone with his third pitch: 2 and 1. Righetti returned with a fast ball to the outside of the plate part of the plate. Rance doubled it hard over Billy Sample's head in left field. Iorg scored from first, and Whitt went to third. Fernandez hit an infield single when he pulled a hard ground ball to Mattingly, who had to dive for it. There was no play at first base. That loaded the bases for Moseby, who singled, driving in Ernie and Rance. The score was 5-3.

Billy Martin called for his second bullpen ace, Brian Fisher.

photograph Canada Wide/The Toronto Sun

Dave Winfield is upset as he's called out at second by umpire
Ted Hendry September 12. The Yankees beat Toronto 7-5.

Billy did not seem to have confidence in his other relievers. Righetti and Fisher had done a great job for the Yankees all year long, and Billy knew he had to stop the Blue Jays at any cost. Right-hander Brian Fisher's first batter was Cliff Johnson, our DH. Clifford has a thing about runners in scoring positions. "If there's a man on second and third, and nobody out, or only one out, somebody's going to be touching home plate." Saturday night was no different. He hit Brian Fisher's first pitch for a line drive, base hit to centre field, scoring two runs. Cliff had come through once again. He is a great clutch hitter, no doubt about it.

The whole night was a great night for Blue Jay hitters: Moseby had 3 hits with 2 RBIs; Cliff went 2 for 4 with 2 RBIs; Barfield had 2 for 5 with a big home run; Garth Iorg, filling in at second for Garcia, who was injured, was 3 for 4; and Rance had 2 RBIs, one the game-winning double to left. All in all a great performance by everyone. We had a two game edge in the series, heading into the final game on Sunday.

I was in the broadcast booth on Saturday evening when I noticed George Steinbrenner ranting and raving about Mary O'Dowd, the singer who had come to grief with her rendition of "O Canada." "Never again! Never again! It's either you," George hollered, pointing to the organist, "or Merrill. That's all. Nobody else! Who is this Mary O'Dowd anyway?" Steinbrenner was totally embarrassed. He wanted everything done perfectly. He is a very successful businessman. He has put some great teams on the field. He had an idea of how things should be done, and he wanted them done that way.

Later on Steinbrenner called Dave Winfield, *Mr. May*, and allowed as how he felt the Yankees should have Reggie Jackson (*Mr. October*) back again. What kind of thinking prompted that? George knew that his players would hear about the comment. Every reporter and media type in New York waits with baited breath for George to loose another volley at the Yankees. Steinbrenner, when he made the statement he did, must not have cared very much about the effect it would have in the clubhouse, and on Billy Martin. He said, in essence, his team could not win. It was a terrible thing to say at a time like that. The Yankees had only lost two games out of four. They still had a reasonable chance of splitting the series, or holding the Blue Jays' lead to two and one half games. George Steinbrenner's comments Saturday night un-

Tony Fernandez and George Bell collide in Exhibition
Stadium's shallow centre field as they chase Bill Buckner's hit
September 25. Boston beat Toronto 4-2.

doubtedly put his players in the worst frame of mind possible for a come back.

• • • •

Game Four matched Doyle Alexander against Ed Whitson. Doyle was magnificent throughout the second half of the season, and he was flawless in Sunday's game. He allowed one hit through the first six innings; he was as believable and as smooth as he ever has been. The Blue Jays scored six runs in the third inning, as Doyle notched his 16th victory, 8-5. When Doyle walked off the field, for a reliever, late in the game, Yankee fans gathered behind the dugout to taunt him, as they do with all players. Doyle looked them over, tilted his head back, and smiled, "Not today, boys. Not today!"

This pretty much summed up the whole series for us. We went four and a half games ahead. We went to the Big Apple, right into "the lion's den," and, after a shakey beginning (a six-run seventh inning in Game One), we showed our true mettle by winning three in a row. The Yankees were on a skid, helped along, in my opinion, by the public outbursts of their owner.

There was and is a dramatic difference between the two organizations, between George Steinbrenner and Peter Hardy: one wanted attention, wanted to run the whole show all the time; the other fought to get the best out of his people, to develop a good relationship with the players and with their community. George Steinbrenner wants production. He wants to win at all costs. That is probably the right attitude for New York City. I prefer Peter Hardy's approach. The Blue Jays acquire good, young people and stick with them; they let their players know they have confidence in them. Peter Hardy has good judgement, and he is patient. He gives his club a good, professional, working atmosphere.

As we made our way to the bus on Sunday afternoon, Thursday and the crowd yelling "Sweep, sweep, sweep! You guys are choking. We are catching you. We'll be in first place by the end of the series." seemed an eternity away. Sunday afternoon was warm and very quiet. There was a loud boo everytime a Yankee player came out of the clubhouse. We even heard an occasional "Way to go, Blue Jays!" and were mightily impressed at the audacity of those Blue Jay fans who had come to cheer us on in the midst of the disappointed New Yorkers.

CHAPTER 9

Spoilers

WHEN THE BLUE JAYS MET THE DETROIT TIGERS FOR A THREE-game series in Detroit October 1 - 3, we knew the Tigers' main role against us would be as spoilers. Detroit had had an off year; they did have the opportunity to finish third in the Eastern Division, but after that, the most they could hope for was to slow us down, upset us a bit and keep the Blue Jays from clinching the pennant in Detroit.

We had an off day on Monday, prior to the series. We'd swept three games in Milwaukee, getting 22 hits and 13 runs on Sunday. We had a lot of momentum going, and that off day probably cost us.

I spent Monday night with my wife, Jimmy Key and his wife and Ron Musselman and his wife, as we all had a nice relaxing dinner at a Japanese steakhouse. We ran into Johnny Grubb and his wife, and all exchanged greetings and wishes of good luck. Johnny asked about my ankle, and I told him it was coming along well, that there was an outside chance I could play.

We went back to the hotel, down to the lounge and a big-screen TV to watch Monday night football, and hoping to get a glimpse of the Yankees' score — they were playing Balti-more. The California Angels were playing the Kansas City Royals in a big 4-game series; both were tied up in that series, although the Angels eventually beat Kansas City, taking a 1-game lead. The Yankees' score never came up on the scoreboard. Monday night football, of course, is pretty primal stuff, and O.J. Simpson, Joe Namath, and Frank Gifford just never did seem to get around to that baseball score from Yankee Stadium. Finally, we had to go up to our room and turn on ESPN to find out that the Yankees had won again.

We lost half a game by having an off day.

Tuesday afternoon, we had our shares meeting at the hotel. This was a meeting of those 21 players who had been with the Blue Jays from June 1 on. We had to decide what portion the remaining players would share of the World Series/Play-off pool, which is created by 60% of the gate receipts of the first four games of the late championship series, and 60% of the gate receipts of the first four World Series games. The moneys are divided between the winner, the loser, the two divisional losers, the second-place teams, and the third-place teams. A share in 1985 could amount to over $100,000 for a World Series winner. This meeting was very important.

There were 19 players who had been with the team for varying lengths of time throughout the summer. We had to vote on each of them: people like Al Oliver, Len Matuszek, Luis Leal (who started the season and was now back home in Venezuela), Mitch Webster, Henke, Filer, Fielder, Davis, Hearron, Johnson, all those people who joined the club in August or September and played vital roles on the baseball team. We had to apportion their shares. The meeting went very well. There were a lot of good arguments in favour of various players and various awards, and I was pleased with the results. Doyle Alexander stayed around to help me write it out and make sure I had the language correct.

I didn't arrive at the ballpark until 5:20 and I had to hustle right into my workout. The excitement around the ball club was evident. The Yankees were going to play Milwaukee, but we didn't think Milwaukee had a chance of winning, particularly because they had mounted such a feeble offence against us.

Doyle Alexander was starting for us against Frank Tanana, the left-hander who had joined the Tigers at mid-season. Tanana had been pitching well. He is a breaking-ball pitcher who also has an off-speed fast ball, but not a lot of velocity.

Frank does have pinpoint control, however, and he can move the ball in and out, changing speeds, with great skill.

The Blue Jays are basically a fast-ball club: our hitters are aggressive and thrive on a diet of fast balls. Controlled off-speed pitches and change-ups can shut us down.

Detroit's Darrell Evans, the American league home-run leader, knocked two home runs off Doyle Alexander, and that was enough to win the game for Detroit. The Yankees won again as well.

The atmosphere in the clubhouse was good after the game. We had just been beaten. Garth Iorg said he felt the game was the best one he had ever seen Tanana pitch, and his victory that night gave him four in a row.

Wednesday night we were still relaxed. It looked as if Milwaukee wasn't going to beat the Yankees, but we kept hoping that Brewer left-hander Teddy Higuera, the Mexican rookie who was having a fantastic year with a poor ball club (14 wins), might pull out a miracle. Dave Stieb went against Jack Morris for game number two of our series. Stieb and Morris have a kind of silent rivalry. Regarded as two of the top right-handers in the American league, they're quite competitive with one another.

I'm sitting in the training room before the game. Garcia is lying on the bench. He won't play: he's got somewhat of a bad knee and doesn't move well. Bobby Cox is going with Garth Iorg, who is hot right now and swinging the bat very well. Stieb comes in. He's nervous, walking around the trainer's room waiting to get his arm rubbed by Kenny Carson before he goes out to warm up. He's always been troubled by a tender elbow, but it's never stopped him from pitching. "When are you going to win another game?" asks Garcia. "There's no way Morris is going to beat me tonight," Stieb answers, and he laughs, jokes and half-kiddingly says, "I'll get 'em."

The match-up went well early on. Morris has a fast ball and a very effective split-fingered fork ball, which acts like a sinker ball with three quarters of the fast-ball velocity. Stieb gave up a homer to Evans, Evans 40th, making him the first man to hit 40 home runs in both leagues. (He is also the oldest man, at 37, to win a home run-crown). Kirk Gibson followed with a towering drive off the centre-field fence, over Moseby's head, for an inside-the-park home run. Al Oliver and I were sitting next to each other on the bench, and he turned to me, "Do you know, when that ball hit the centre-field fence, Gibson was almost to second base?"

The final score was Detroit 4, Blue Jays 2; but Teddy Higuera did manage to beat the Yankees, 1 - 0, in a great game, and our magic number fell to two. Any combination of Yankee losses and/or Blue Jay wins which added up to 2 meant that we would clinch the pennant.

Wednesday's game featured Jim Clancy going against Walt Terrill. Terrill is a sinker-ball pitcher who really pitched well in Tiger Stadium in 1985. He was acquired from the Mets, and picked up the slack from Milt Wilcox, who missed most of the year with a bad arm. Our guys seemed exceptionally loose. There were stereos blasting away in the clubhouse, and Al Oliver brought his tape recorder with the song "Ain't No Stopping Us Now." That seemed to be everybody's attitude. All we needed was one more game. No matter what the Yankees did, if we could win one in Detroit, we'd clinch or tie.

The media was looking for a clubhouse celebration, too. They were in all day long, moving things about, hooking up lights, stretching microphone cables all over, taping up lockers. They were setting the scene for a real party.

There was a lot of laughing and joking. Lou Thornton kept talking about driving his "drop-top" dream Mercedes down in Hope Hull, Alabama in the winter. Moseby sat in front of his locker talking about how he was "ready tonight! Ain't no stopping me tonight!" He got up and leaned against a floodlight standard above his locker and began to practise his post-game interview: "Well it's been a great season for us. Yeah, I know I hit 3 home runs tonight, but it was really a team effort. This is a great team, and we've really struggled hard, and battled tough all year long. It's very gratifying to win the pennant here in Detroit. . . ." He went on and on, not speaking to anyone in particular. What confidence! It was fun to watch him — 25 years old, just starting on a career that promises to be a lengthy and successful one.

I sat in the trainers' room peering through the mesh fence separating it from the clubhouse, and I thought, "I hope Lloyd gets the chance to give that speech tonight. It'll take a lot of the pressure off everyone."

Pressure. Everybody used that word. There was no

pressure. We just went out and played good baseball. There was no pressure at all. We simply had to play well. Guys at the plate were struggling a bit. Mulliniks was not swinging the bat well; he was jumping at the ball and needed to smooth his swing out again. Nor had Johnson gotten back on track with us yet, but then he had not had the opportunity to hit the way he did everyday for us in 1983 and 1984, and for the Rangers in the first half of 1985. Al Oliver was not hitting up to his capabilities either. George Bell was really struggling: he had been hampered by nagging injuries, some of them from that collision with Fernandez in Toronto when they both went after that shallow fly ball in left field. George was trying to adjust his body; he was not staying back on the ball, but tended to drift out in front. We needed to have George Bell get hot.

Talk flew around the clubhouse. "O.K., boys, tonight just line drives. All we gotta do is hit line drives. Nobody has to hit home runs. We get 20 line drives tonight, 20 singles, we'll score some runs. Runs are at a premium right now. A couple here. A couple there . . . we'd have won the first two games!"

You couldn't really say our backs were against the wall. We still had three games with the Yankees, and we were still four games ahead. The Yankees had to win them all; we would have to lose every game. Fine. Still, a win in Detroit would be very nice.

Clancy was flawless through the early part of the game. There was no problem in the first, second, third innings. He had good fast balls, change-ups, and sliders thrown for strikes. Then he walked himself into trouble in the fourth: Grubb, and Nelson Simmons on. Two on, no outs. Alan Trammel hit a ground ball which looked like a double play, but hustled double quick down to first base and beat it out. One out. Men at first and third. Tom Brookens was the batter. He hit a Clancy hang slider into right centre field for a triple, and drove in two runs. That was all the Tigers would need.

Bobby Cox pulled Clancy, who made a good effort but had one bad pitch. Gary Lavelle came on and pitched effectively until his fourth batter when something snapped in his elbow. He would be finished for the season.

Detroit had effectively shut the door on the Blue Jays.

CHAPTER 10

Clinching the Pennant

THE NEW YORK YANKEES CAME TO TORONTO OCTOBER 4, 5, AND 6 for the final game of the series. All we had to do was win one game, and the excitement in the clubhouse was rampant, as many of the players arrived early for Friday night's game. Everyone was laughing and joking. The media people were trying to prepare the scene once again for a "spontaneous" celebration, should we clinch the pennant that night. I felt a little uneasy because it all seemed too elaborate, too planned. I could hear Yogi Berra in my mind again and again, "It's not over till it's over."

The Blue Jay coaches, managers and trainers all seemed to be really tense, perhaps because the players were so confident. We'd played well all year long and no one wanted to see it slip away from us now.

Bobby Cox held a brief meeting before the game, nothing serious. "Don't worry about a thing. You guys are playing well. We're proud of you; the organization is proud of you; the City of Toronto is behind you 100%. Just go out there and have a good series. Go out there and play. Everybody's free swinging. Turn the bats loose!" As he dismissed the meeting, Bobby made one final request, "All pitchers report tomorrow at 4:30," for batting practice.

Everyone laughed because tomorrow, Saturday, was a day

game and everyone would be at the ballpark at 10:30; by 4:30 we'd be deep in the middle of the game. I turned to Doyle and we both exclaimed simultaneously, "There's no pressure here!"

Friday night's game was a good match-up — Jimmy Key and Ed Whitson, the Yankees' right-hander. Whitson was coming off the much-publicized fight with Billy Martin in Baltimore, and I was really surprised to see Martin start him. Everyone knew the two were not on the best of terms. Whitson pitched some pretty good ball games, but we beat him in New York in the last meeting of these two teams. I thought Billy Martin was going to announce Whitson and then bring on someone else. Billy will do anything he needs to do to win.

The game was scoreless until the fourth inning when the Yankees put two on the board. The rains came after the third out in the top of the fourth. Just what we needed. We wanted to come right back with our offence, but Davey Phillips, the umpire behind the plate, motioned to the grounds crew to cover the field. All we had to do was hurry up and wait.

Just 59 minutes later, when we finally got back to playing, the Blue Jays put two runs of their own on the board on Andre Robertson's error. The park came alive. It looked as if every single one of the 47,000 plus fans was on his feet as we tied up the ball game 2 - 2. Later on Moseby walked and Iorg laid down a beautiful sacrifice bunt. Yankees' third baseman Pagliarulo and first baseman Mattingly came charging hard, but Iorg deadened Scurry's curve ball and advanced Mosby to second. Cliff Johnson came up. I'd picked Cliff earlier on as my hero for the game. He was overmatched his first two at bats, and tried to swing too hard. Here, though, Cliff came up with a ground-ball base hit up the middle to Bobby Meacham, who knocked it down. Moseby, hustling all the way from second base, scored as Meacham's throw went wide of the plate. It was 3-2 for Blue Jays and the crowd went crazy.

Tom Henke was on the mound, and we led with one run going into the top of the ninth. The Blue Jays' bench was supercharged: Jimmy Key kept clapping his hands as he walked up and down the dugout; some of the rookies sat quietly, anticipating the moment when we would all run ecstatically out to the mound.

Henke got the first batter in the ninth to pop up; then he

struck out Willie Randolph. One more out and we could pop the cork. Butch Wynegar was the batter. Jim Acker, sitting next to me on the bench, was a nervous wreck. Iorg must have walked three miles back and forth to the clubhouse, "Man, I can't stand this. This is just too much." The excitement of the crowd was phenomenal. Wynegar, normally a left-handed hitter, also has the ability to switch hit. Henke built him up to a full count.

With two outs, leading 3-2, Ernie Whitt and Henke were both trying to pitch Wynegar away. We knew he was a low fast-ball hitter, who liked the ball on the inside half of the plate, where his power is. Henke was caught up in the enthusiasm of the game. He tried to over-throw the ball and put a little bit more on it than his natural stuff. When he did that, the ball lost a little velocity because the tension in Tom's hand slowed his arm down; the ball didn't release as well and it came over the plate, drifting back to the middle of the plate. When that happened, Butch put the big part of the bat on the ball. It was a nice easy swing. Everybody turned their heads, saying, "My God, that ball jumped off his bat!"

A home run. The score was tied.

Butch did not have a chance to play too much in 1985 and as I talked to him on Saturday morning, he said, "I just didn't want to be the one that made the last out to end our Pennant chances. It's been a miserable year for me. . . ." He had been hit in the head with a line drive in the on-deck circle, was put on the disabled list, and had had nagging injuries all year long. Eventually Hassey took over his job, because Hassey was a regular left-handed hitter. If I had to pick someone on the Yankees to whom we were going to give up a home run, Butch Wynegar would be my candidate. He's a helluva young guy; he and I have tracked along the same paths throughout our careers.

Henke was upset. He knew that he had made a bad pitch. He said, "Geez, I was trying to throw it outside and I got it back over the plate too much." Normally, Tom is a very confident young man. He goes out there with the attitude, "Give me the ball, I'll see what I can do."

Later on in the inning, Moseby dropped a routine fly ball hit by Mattingly and allowed Bobby Meacham to score from second base. The Yankees won 4-3. Two of our most confident people happened to have one of the roughest games in

photograph courtesy The Hamilton Spectator

Lloyd Moseby in a pensive mood.

their careers that day. It was a depressing time for all of us, and there were a lot of deep sighs in the clubhouse.

I sat on the bench and watched the players go inside, some of them voicing their disbelief in what had happened. George Bell sat down next to me and said, "Now, do we have to win two?" "No, George," I replied, "we don't have to win two. All we need is one. We've got three games left: two with the Yankees, and possibly one with the Orioles on Monday, if we need it. You don't get penalized for losing a game like this. You still have to win only one." It's amazing how guys have different concepts about what it takes to win a pennant. The magic number really seems to be a baffling thing for many of the players. They don't understand it.

I sat there trying to gather my thoughts as to what I would say about the game. "There will be a tomorrow." That is what I talked about with Scott Ferguson after the game, that and the fact that it was a good ball game. Both clubs played well. We didn't expect to lose on a drop fly ball, that's for sure. But we had Doyle Alexander pitching on Saturday, and we'd have to come back. The Blue Jays are a resilient club; they've got a lot of character. They would bounce back with the same enthusiasm another day. There did not seem to be much more to do than go home, put the game behind us, and think about tomorrow.

I ran into Jim Acker later on in the clubhouse.

"I caught him, I caught him!" he said.

"What are you talking about?"

"I went into the clubhouse during the game to get some coffee and, as I was going through, I noticed Jimy Williams sitting in front of his locker, staring inside. . . . He was drinking out of a bottle. I looked at him and it was a bottle of Malox. Nerves are churning. Pennant race . . . it's great."

• • • •

A little digression about Canadian fans: when you talk about the intelligence level of baseball fans, you get into a very, very controversial area. Baseball fans differ radically as you go around the league.

When I first came to Toronto, I came from Milwaukee. Milwaukee fans are "Let's go to the ball park and have a beer, and take our shirts off, and see if we can scream at the opposition and really have a great time. See how many beer cups we can stack up in the bleachers" folks. They come out in April and take their shirts off because it's baseball season — it's supposed to be warm. They don't care what the temperature is, but they're going to drink a lot of beer and sing the old "Roll Out the Barrel" song and have a great time. That's what we would see in Milwaukee — party time from the moment you got there to when its all over. They have tailgate parties outside the park; they come inside and drink their beer; and they stand up from the opening pitch until the last out of the game and cheer their Brewers.

Toronto is different, and my wife, Arlene especially, noticed the difference as she sat in the stands. Early Toronto fans would watch, look around, applaud once in a while, and act very civilized. They did not really get involved in the old excitement of the game. Naturally, back then, there wasn't a whole lot of excitement for the Blue Jays because they were a bad team — and there wasn't any beer either! The pitchers didn't play very well, and the fans couldn't even drown their sorrows in a beer or two.

As the team got better, fans' interest perked up. And we found out more about the history of Toronto Blue Jay sports fans. Toronto fans seem hooked on tradition. They've been disappointed over the years; their Leafs dominated hockey for many years — now wins are a rarity. The fans still go out; they still fill the hockey arena. They have a stoical "I can't believe you've done this to me, Leafs. I'm going to come out because I know there's such history in the club that you must win sooner or later" approach. They won't give up that Leaf tradition. As the Blue Jays progressed and became more competitive, the fans started getting more and more excited. They learned more and more about when and how to cheer.

I've always said Blue Jay fans really became fans when they began to boo! When the Jays were expected to win, were supposed to win, . . . fans would boo us if we lost. That's when I knew we had baseball fans in Toronto. They always booed the opposition — with vigor! They would boo Reggie Jackson and they'd boo Billy Martin, when these people came to town, because they read in the newspaper these were the bad guys, and you're supposed to boo the bad guys. When Toronto began to boo Dave Stieb, Lloyd Moseby and everybody else on the Jays team when they made mistakes on the field, I knew that Toronto fans had arrived. They were going to come out and support the team, and if we performed well they were going to respond well.

We could sense this support earlier on when the fans began to chant, hollering for Ernie Whitt, with "Ernie . . . Ernie . . . Ernie. . . ." This was obviously an adaptation from the "Ar-gos" chant so often shouted at the Argo games and still shouted even at the earlier Blue Jay games. Luckily, now, no one says anything about the Argos at Blue Jay games. The fans wouldn't put up with it. They're the Blue Jay fans and very protective of their Blue Jays. Blue Jay fans have become the classiest fans in the American League, in my mind. They love their team, but they respect great performances by either team. They boo when the home boys let them down; but they quickly forgive and forget as they did with Moseby and his dropped fly ball. They come back and support us again and again.

When the Yankees came to town, after all the incidents in Yankee Stadium with the Canadian national anthem, Toronto fans applauded the American national anthem, a very respectable, sincere applause. That showed class. When they cheered wildly for "O' Canada", that showed their pride and love for Canada, Toronto and the Blue Jays.

Toronto fans were disappointed about the Friday night game against the New York Yankees, but no one left. Fans had traditionally gotten up and walked out of any game in order to catch the subway at a particular time — no matter what the score. New players come to Toronto and are shocked to see their fans leave in the eighth or ninth inning of a tie game. But on Friday night, nobody left his seat. It rained and was raining all through the course of the game but nobody left. Those people had been there before; they had sat through snowstorms, and windstorms, fog, cold, and seagull attacks and more. They were not going to leave. They wanted to be there when the Blue Jays finally won the American League East. At the end of the Friday night game, they all sat in disbelief.

And then Saturday they came back once again.

• • • •

I was the first one in the clubhouse Saturday morning because I needed to get my rehab done before gametime. I felt a lot of concern and disappointment after Friday's game.

103

Doyle Alexander, hoisted upon the shoulders of Jim Acker
and Billy Caudill, celebrates his pennant-clinching victory over
New York October 5.

The players might even react unfavourably to what had happened, especially because Moseby had come in after the game commenting to the press, "I blew it! I just missed it." He left the clubhouse fairly quick after that.

I wanted to be there early to get my work done, and so I would be in the clubhouse when the players started coming in. Jim Acker is always there early, and he came in a little after me. We sat around. Nobody really talked about what had happened the night before. We had a big job ahead of us, to win the game on Saturday. I think the biggest thing in our favour was Doyle Alexander. He had pitched in clinching games before, and he has had a great career in Toronto. Ever since he joined us, Doyle has been the steadiest pitcher we've had on the staff. We knew that Doyle would keep us in the ball game. He would do *something* to keep us in the ball game.

Going out on the field for batting practice, everyone noticed that the wind was howling in from left field. Doyle always asks, when the hitters come back off the field, "How's the ball carrying? Where's it carrying? Is it carrying to left, or is it carrying to right?" He wanted to know who would have the best advantage at the plate that night, the right-handers or the left-handers. Saturday, Doyle knew that he would have Mattingly, Ron Hassey and Pagliarulo to contend with; the good left-handed hitters could reach the fence in right field. Nobody had a chance in left field. The wind was blowing in so hard that it would take a rocket to launch the ball out of there. Once Alexander knew about the wind, he had his game plan. He would pitch the left-handers away. Any inside fast ball he threw them during the course of the game would be inside off the plate. He didn't want to throw anything at all on the inside half of the plate. The ball was going to be out of the strike zone, or it was going to be a fast ball away. Batters would have to pull the ball, and when they did that, they hit on the ground or weakly to left field.

At noon that day, Al Oliver, who was sitting next to me in the locker room, said, "Man, we gotta win this one today. We don't want to come back here tomorrow and be left with one game and have a one-game lead. We gotta win this game today." Everbody was upbeat. Moseby and Upshaw were exchanging barbs about who's going to make it: "No, it's going to be my turn." "No, I can handle it, don't worry about that." Doyle had gone to the bull pen to warm up. The rest of

Toronto fans have something to cheer about as their Blue Jays
clinch the American league East October 5

the players gathered in the locker room 25 minutes or so before the game and began to limber up. They were scattered around the room, doing stretching exercises, relaxing, giving each other a little bit of jab here and there, trying to make everybody relax. Everyone was loose before the game.

As the announcer began introducing the players after the national anthems, the fans went berserk. They had put Friday night behind them, had come back anew, with one thing in mind: Beat the Yankees. When Moseby, the second player out, was introduced, the fans gave him a rousing welcome. They had remembered that he is a leader, one of the keys of our ball club, and they had forgiven him overnight.

Early in the game, Ernie Whitt hit our first home run. The Blue Jays took the lead. Later, Moseby and Upshaw hit back-to-back home runs. Our momentum grew slowly. We did not have the excitement of Friday night when Moseby scored from second base on Cliff Johnson's ground ball. That totally animated celebration in the dugout as the run scored had gone. Now we were matter-of-fact. "Great job, Ernie! Way to hit the ball, Ernie! Atta way to get things going! Come on, guys, let's hit some more!" No one said, "This was gonna do it." We knew that we had to play until the last out was made. We had learned a valuable lesson on Friday night, and on Saturday no one got overly excited about the fact that we had a three run lead after three home runs. Later as we went along, a slow, very controlled pattern of excitement began to develop.

Bobby Cox was at the back of the dugout, standing in the back tunnel. Bobby is very superstitious. If we aren't scoring runs, he'll move to different spots in the dugout. His normal managerial spot is on the closest end of the dugout to home plate, but, as the game progresses, if we aren't scoring, Bobby keeps changing places. If we score two or three runs from a particular spot, while Bobby is standing or sitting there, he'll be back in that same spot for the next inning. This time, Bobby was down in the tunnel, looking out to the field. Occasionally, he would ask Jim Acker, "What's happened? What's the count?" As the Blue Jays scored runs to take the lead, Bobby continued to stay in that spot. He remained there throughout the course of the game.

Ron Hassey came to bat with two out in the top of the ninth. Billy Caudill was sitting on my left, Acker on my right.

photograph by Neal Sadja

Toronto Blue Jays coaches Cito Gaston (batting) and Al Widmar (pitching) with Walter Stancheson (umpire's room attendent).

No one had said anything about winning until two outs were registered on the board. Then Acker turned to Caudill and said, "Let's carry him off the field! Let's carry him off the field!" Doyle had pitched a great game. Caudill said, "O.K., I'll meet you right there." We knew there was going to be mass confusion on the field when the game ended and the fans came out. There was simply no way of keeping them off the field. I thought "How in the world am I going to get out there before the crowd gets out there?" I was still limping and hobbling. . . . Hassey popped up to left field. George Bell positioned himself under the ball, made the catch, went down to his knees and put his arms up in the air.

Everybody exploded out of the dugout. It was a tremendous feeling. I was caught up with excitement and had tears in my eyes at the same time. I had gone through this before, but never with this full, total appreciation of the moment. We had won a Pennant! We had come from last place to first place. We had been selected in spring training as the best team in baseball by several people, and we had vindicated that selection.

I hustled out on the field, as Acker and Caudill got to Doyle and lifted him up on their arms. Doyle is not a very excitable person, but you could see his emotions as he raised thumbs up to the crowd. Doyle's happiness was passed on to the rest of the players. They take a lot of pride in Doyle, because he is such a great pitcher. They know what he's been through with the Yankees, with Steinbrenner, and with New York City. Doyle is a country boy from Alabama now living in Texas. On the Toronto team, he's gotten a new opportunity, and he's pitched very well as a result.

Seeing Doyle Alexander riding around, on the shoulders of the players struck a familiar chord in me. When I came to Toronto, nobody else wanted me. Toronto was my last stop. I had to resurrect my career, or be out of baseball. Everything that has happened in Toronto has been fabulous for me. I think Doyle would say the same thing. There weren't many stops left for him when he arrived, but Doyle has restored his career: he's back on top.

As we moved off the field and through the throng of fans, everyone kept slapping each other on the back, hugging and congratulating each other. The champagne was flowing when we hit the clubhouse. There was a make-shift stage set up in

photograph by Dan Hamilton

Arlene & I celebrating as the Blue Jays clinched the pennant, and women were allowed in the Clubhouse for the first time.

the middle of the room; trash cans full of ice cold champagne stood right beside it. Everybody grabbed the champagne and started to spray it around. It was obvious that the kids — Manny Lee and Lou Thornton had thought about this celebration for a long time. They were popping corks, spraying everybody, chortling, enjoying every moment. Some of the other guys were more laid back, savouring the importance of our win. Cliff Johnson gave me a big hug and said, "Man, this is what we all play for."

Cito Gaston couldn't stop crying. Cito had paid his dues as a player, and as a coach. He'd suffered all year long with his hitters when they were criticized for not hitting. He had worked hard and long with each of us, and he took our slumps personally. "Man," he said, "This is great! If I can stop crying, I'm really going to have fun!"

While Fergie Oliver and Ken Singleton were standing on the stage doing TV interviews with the players, I went over to the trash can and grabbed a couple of bottles of the champagne. Early on, I had made a promise to Arlene that, should we ever had have the chance to win a pennant again, she and I would dance on the dugout together. Moving towards the dugout, I noticed the main doors had already been locked. "I gotta get back out there," I told a member of the grounds crew. "You don't want to go back out there, man, it's crazy out there!" he replied. I was going back out regardless of the pandemonium, so they opened the door to the umpire's runway, and I walked out to the crowd. Naturally, once the fans saw a player (and it did not make a difference who it was), they went bananas and started tugging on my champagne bottles. "No, don't take these away from me. This is a special moment."

I looked for Arlene but couldn't see her. I kept looking in the stands. Finally I glanced over towards the dugout. There she was! I walked up onto the roof, quietly put my arms around her, gave her a big kiss, and said, "We did it! We've done it again!" and passed her the champagne. Arlene popped the cork, spraying everyone in front of her. Pam Cox, Patty Iorg, Diana Caudill and several other wives were also there. Oh, how great it was to be able to celebrate once again. Everybody had grown up with the team, and we were all very relieved to have finally won at last.

I had to go back to the clubhouse, and by the time I had

Jimy Williams and his wife Peggy

gotten inside, all hell had broken loose. The media and front office people, Paul Beeston and Pat Gillick, were all there. Beeston was congratulating players, and had his Labatts in hand.

Doyle Alexander had already left. He had received his traditional shower of champagne, grabbed a couple of cold beers, and gone off to ice his arm because, as a consummate pro, he knew there were more games to be played.

The celebration continued, and all of a sudden, we looked up to see our wives coming into the clubhouse. Oh fabulous day! Paul Beeston had invited them in to share the moment. Even Ernie's kids came in. I looked at Arlene as Pam Cox and Jeannie Mulliniks arrived. "We made it! We're not only in the Championship, but my God, we're in the clubhouse too!" she said. There was more champagne, and I gave Arlene another big hug and a kiss.

Pam Cox went over to Bobby. They threw their arms around one another, and you could see their joy.

Most of the team, including the coaches ate, drank, and danced the rest of the night away at the Copa. It was a grand celebration, a happy time. And, who knows, maybe we set a precedent: wives in the clubhouse for victory celebrations. I think it is an idea whose time has come. I hope so. I'm all for it.

CHAPTER 11

Dave Stieb

DAVE STIEB IS A TREMENDOUSLY COMPETITIVE PERSON. HE'S always been highly successful in his athletic career, be it baseball or football or whatever, in high school or in college. He was an all-American outfielder in Southern Illinois and, when he got up to the Blue Jays, he was obviously promoted before he really had become an accomplished major leaguer. Dave didn't deserve to pitch in the major leagues so early on in his career. He was 10-and-2 in the minor leagues. Once with the Blue Jays, however, Stieb acquired instant stardom because the team didn't have anything else to promote. He was their Number One prospect; he wasn't a star, but they were going to promote him and make him the Number One Star. The Blue Jays set out to utilize some of his potential and turn him into a star prematurely. This may well have had an adverse effect on Stieb, who was and still is a young man. He became very intense and very determined to be the best every time he stepped on the mount.

Initially, Dave was not capable of being the best. He had a lot of ability physically. The club behind him didn't have as much. Dave couldn't accept the fact that the Blue Jays could not score runs, or could not catch the ball or could not make the plays behind him. This bothered him to the point where he would begin to say things. People turned off to Dave Stieb.

I still feel he wasn't malicious, but rather intense. He would come off the field and say, "My God, how could you miss that ball!" before he could think about it. And if the player to whom the accusation was addressed did not hear, his team mates did, and the statement would be repeated. Blue Jay's players began to feel intensely about Stieb: "Well, who does he think he is? We're trying just as hard as he is." I don't think it was malicious, I just think it was his intensity.

I believe this is still happening, although to a lesser extent. Dave Stieb now has a good accomplished team behind him.

After the second game of the Boston series, Bill Buckner said that most of the hitters in the American League despise Dave Stieb, and they all go up there trying to hit him. What Buck meant is that when Stieb stands out on the mound, he is totally different from when he's not on the mound. He goes out there and he's in his own little world. He believes that nobody should hit him. Well, that's great. A lot of pitchers feel that way. How the opposition perceives this attitude is a different story. Doyle Alexander feels that no one should hit him, too. He just pitches and gets the outs, walks off the field and it's over. When Stieb gives up a hit, he fires the rosin bag down and stares at the batter on first base as if to say: "How in the world can you hit that? You don't have the ability to be able to hit me." Stieb doesn't actually think this way, but it is the way he comes across. He looks on the mound, throws the rosin down, and he's talking to himself all the time saying "That was a terrible pitch" or "How in the world did he hit that one? He hit it off the end of the bat and it's a base hit. . . ." Dave takes everything that happens on the mound personally. "The umpire misses the pitch because he doesn't like me." "The batter gets a hit because it's off the end of his bat and he's just lucky." Dave has to realize that major league players have a lot of ability, and a lot of them, hitters or pitchers, have as much ability as Dave Stieb. We're all equals; some people excel. Dave should excel but he hasn't yet, to my mind.

Dave needs to stand back and look at his ability and say "This is the kind of ability I have. I'm going to use it to win games." He's very happy to lead the league in ERA. He's very happy to be up among the league leaders in strike-outs. He wants to be Number One; he wants to be the best. He hasn't realized yet how to become the best. If we put Doyle Alex-

photograph by Neal Sadja

Dave Stieb living it up with his agent Bob LaMonte

ander's head on Dave Stieb's arm, we might easily win 35 games.

All through this year and probably every year that Stieb has pitched for the Jays, one thing runs true: not enough runs were scored for him. There's a lot of talk about Dave not getting a lot of support. The Blue Jays do not get a lot of runs when he pitches. This is not, however, in my view a result of players' indifference to hitting when Stieb's around. That doesn't happen. Players are selfish. They're individuals. They go out there for one reason: they're going to do well for themselves, and that is reflected by the team doing well. We're going to try to score as many runs as we can. I don't think anybody thinks that "I'm not going to play hard today because Dave's pitching." We know darn well that when Dave's on the mound, we've got a chance to win the game. I don't care who we're playing, or who's pitching against us.

One theory I have about the reason Stieb doesn't get an awful lot of runs scored is the fact that the other pitcher knows he's got to pitch his ass off. Other managers know they're going to have to scratch for runs; they bunt a little more, they sacrifice, they hit and run, they steal bases, they take a little bit more aggressive approach to playing against Dave, because he can shut them out any day. I think that the opposition says to itself, "We have to score as many runs as we can, and every one that we can, against Stieb. We can't give him anything." The defence knows, "We can't give him anything. We've got to hustle and get the fly balls, and cut off the ground balls and make the plays," because Dave is always tough.

Everybody wants to beat Stieb. Stieb has been successful; Stieb has pitched in All-Star games; Stieb has won All-Star games; Stieb has been a very visible Toronto Blue Jay, even in the years where the Blue Jays were thought of as being an amateur team from the North. Stieb has been out front. He has the image. He's cocky out there. Dave has a lot of confidence. He doesn't have bad feelings about other players. He just wants to beat them. He doesn't think that they're anything less than he is. He doesn't think that way, but I know it doesn't come across that way when people watch him on TV or read about him in the paper.

Basically, Dave Stieb is a shy person who doesn't like to be around crowds. He doesn't speak at functions and banquets, because he's uncomfortable doing so. A lot of people don't understand this: if you can play baseball in front of 47,000 people, you ought to be able to go out and talk to a handful of fans. Some people can't or just aren't comfortable. I think this causes Dave a lot of anguish.

Dave Stieb now knows that he has one of the best fielding teams in baseball behind him; and I think he's starting to realize that if he goes over and says to Tony Fernandez, "Great play, Tony," that'll be great for Tony. Tony might even make a more exciting play for him the next inning. I think Dave is learning that and this is a change.

When Fernandez had that horrible two-error inning behind Stieb in New York, Stieb threw down the rosin bag as hard as I've ever seen him throw it down. I joined the club in New York that Friday night and I told Dave "If you had thrown baseballs as hard as you had thrown the rosin bag, then you wouldn't have lost the game."

"What do you mean?"

"Well, I saw you pitching last night on TV, and you were just nit-picking, pitching to the corners and everything else." (Dave and I have advanced in our relationship where I can tell him just what I think.)

He said, "Well, what do you mean?" I said, "It looked like you were scared out there. You walked seven guys." He says, "No, I was just trying to make good pitches."

Well, trying to make good pitches and being scared are real close. Obviously Dave is not scared. No one playing in the major leagues is scared. But Dave was cautious, and he doesn't have to pitch cautiously with his ability; he should pitch aggressively taking it right to them every time he steps on the mound. During that New York game, I think Dave's disgust was not so much at Fernandez' errors as it was at the seven walks. When he fired down the rosin bag, he'd just given up his seventh walk to his last batter. He was out of the game, and he knew that it had slipped away from him.

I really believe Dave Stieb has gone over the hump as far as realizing "These guys behind me are just as good as I am, and I better make sure that I don't upset anyone."

The American League Championship Series

THE FIRST AMERICAN LEAGUE CHAMPIONSHIP GAME IS ABOUT TO be played in Toronto, Canada — a first for the ball club, and a first for the city. October 8, 1985: the Toronto Blue Jays against the Kansas City Royals. This is a culmination of a lot of hard work and that gruelling last week of regular-play baseball when we really tried to clinch the Pennant. The Yankees played "never-die" baseball: they fought back on Friday night, and came back again fighting on Saturday. It was a very tough battle, but we eventually won and clinched.

Now it's Tuesday — an exciting day for everyone on the Blue Jays ball club. We have a lot to be grateful for: we have an opportunity to get into the playoffs and to play a fine team from Kansas City. Dave Stieb is our starting pitcher, and in my mind he can really salvage the season out of this series. He can put the gold dust on his 1985 record of 14-13, which doesn't really reflect his ability. Over and over, I've told Dave to go out there and challenge the hitters to take command of the game, to be an offensive pitcher and go right after the opposition. This is his chance.

We're all anxiously awaiting the game; a lot of the guys have gathered at the ballpark four or five hours ahead of gametime. I go in to Coxie and ask him whether or not I'll be able to stay in the dugout, and even possibly be included at the beginning as the line-ups are being introduced out on the foul lines. It's not much, but I would really feel left out if I couldn't go out there on the foul lines with the rest of the team.

Steib arrives and he's really pretty relaxed. He walks around the clubhouse in his longjohns, talking to everyone. Media people are not allowed in the clubhouse prior to game-time, so we're only players and coaches. We're all relaxed, especially compared to the day before when everybody — all the media — was invited into the clubhouse after our work-out. That had been very hectic with reporters from all over the country converging on all of us in that small area, looking for stories, scoops and different angles — each reporter trying to get a special story. Today, the atmosphere is rather relaxed and friendly.

Acker, Key, Leach and Alexander are playing *Hearts* at the table again. We all want the game to get under way, but nobody is overly nervous about playing. All our pitchers will take batting practice, an anticipatory move for World Series play when American League designated hitters will be dropped. The World Series alternates every other year in this regard in an effort to satisfy both leagues: in '84 the designated-hitter rule was in effect; in '85 it will be omitted. World Series pitchers must hit in 1985.

Blue Jay pitchers, of course, never take batting practice, so today they'll be honing up their bunting and swinging skills — something they don't do very often. (Probably, some of them haven't done so since high school.) The rest of us have fun watching them swing: they get out there and hack, hack away, always talking about what great hitters they were earlier and how they'd really like to go up there and hit. Our pitchers get to home plate and we can immediately see why they're pitchers.

Doyle Alexander is the best hitting pitcher we have. Caudill has a little bit of power. Tom Henke is slotted perfectly for a non-hitter: he's a short-relief man and probably won't ever have to go up to the plate.

Back to the clubhouse. . .

The starting pitchers generally come in later than most of the players. They don't really have to do anything until about

120

7 o'clock or 30 minutes before the game, when they start limbering and loosening up, and move into the trainer's room. Stieb goes in there by himself and sits on the floor, and stretches out his legs — he stands up and stretches around his shoulders and his arm. After about 10 minutes, Kenny Carson will give him a rubdown to loosen up his shoulder and his arm, getting him ready to go out and warm up.

Well, as Stieb is lying on the floor loosening up, George Bell comes into the clubhouse and hollers out, to no one in particular, "Oh my goodness! How that ball is flying out of here tonight!" My eye catches Stieb's eye and we both kind of laugh. Dave says, "Thanks, George, that's just what I wanted to hear." George says, "No — you don't understand. The wind is not blowing at all, but the ball, she's flying!" "Oh, that's great!" Stieb laughs, and he is really pretty relaxed. Then Stieb and Bell get into a mock-argument about whether or not Stieb is going to win tonight. I'm delighted with the way Stieb is in command of himself today. He's relaxed and smiling, making jokes and talking about his wife, Patty, who can't be here, because she's expecting a baby in November and can't fly back and forth for the playoffs. She is at home in Florida.

As he goes out to warm up, Stieb begins to assume his "game face": he wipes the smile off and begins to concentrate. Dave has a lot of determination. He can rise to the occasion like no other player I've seen, and he knows that he must turn it on tonight. Game Number One of any playoff series is very important. It sets the momentum. You want to win, and particularly when you have your best pitcher going. You know that if your man wins tonight, he has the chance to come back and pitch again in Game Number Four or Number Five.

Dave went out on the mound and took total command of the game. He really had everything in order; his fast ball, slider and his change-up. Dave used more fast balls than he does normally. He attacked the hitters; it was as if he said to them, "There's no way you're going to beat me today. This is my game; I'm taking it right here."

Ernie Whitt put us on the board with a base hit through the right side off Charlie Liebrandt. This was all we needed. We held the Royals down until the ninth inning when Tom Henke came on in relief of Stieb, who had pitched a masterful game and left with a 6-0 lead. Coxie put Henke in to make sure he'd keep sharp, to give him a little playoff experience before a really crucial situation in a close ball game. I think it was a great move. Eventually Henke gave up a run, but the fact that he could get those first-game jitters out of the way in a game where we had a sizeable lead was an important factor, one that loomed larger and larger as we moved forward into the playoffs.

The Blue Jays scored two in the second, and three in the third, whereupon Dick Howser pulled out Charlie Liebrandt.

Jimmy Key was charting the game because he would be the starting pitcher in Game Number Two. As Stieb marched his way to a 6-0 lead, Doyle hollered down to Jimmy Key, "Looks like you're pitching on the wrong day, Key; Stieb's taking all your runs." Key laughed back at him, "I don't need but two tomorrow." All the pitchers are always joking about runs, runs, runs . . . how many runs we're going to get.

We won the game 6-1 and we generated a lot of momentum; we won by base hits, step by step, a base hit here, a base hit there; George Bell hustling on a little blooper to left field, beating it into second base for a double and so on.

George set himself a hustler's tempo for this series. He struggled a bit the last month or so of the season, but he was going to make sure he contributed to this championship effort. He scored a big run for us later on in the game on a ball that was hit to the shortstop. George Brett came across, trying to field the ball, and Biancalana threw it to first to retire the batter. Brett had a tough time getting back to the bag. Balboni had to double clutch, trying to get Bell at third base, and when he did that he ended up throwing the ball about 20 feet over Brett's head at third. George Bell was able to score the sixth run of the game.

That game was a great effort by everyone. I think it was a good example of the kind of games we'd played all year long: base hits, good base running, nobody swinging for the fence, just taking what the pitcher will give up (especially a guy like Liebrandt, who moves the ball around so well, changing speeds, throwing little cut-fast balls, sliders inside, and then sinking the ball away from the right-handed hitters). Batters, trying to pull him, get killed. They have to be patient and hit the ball in the opposite way, to stay on him meticulously, not too hard, not too soft, taking what he'll give up.

After the game, the excitement was subdued. We knew we had won a big game. Stieb was outstanding, and this was a great sign for the rest of the pitching staff, knowing that Stieb was back to where he should be.

We wanted to make sure we didn't get carried away. This was only one game, we had to win three more to get to the World Series. We wanted to make sure we didn't lose touch with the fact that we were playing a good ball club in the Royals, and we had to play them tough everyday to win.

● ● ● ●

Game Number Two was Jimmy Key against Buddy Black. Key had pitched so well for us all year long, we felt confident that he'd give us a good effort. Watching him throw earlier on, though, we realized he was having problems with the movement on his tremendous sinker ball. He couldn't get it over the plate and was having trouble with his control. He really wasn't throwing very hard; Jimmy gave up seven hits in just over three innings and threw a total of 78 pitches.

We were down by three runs, when Coxie made the move to go with Dennis Lamp. And what did Lamp do? He retired all 11 men he faced. Lamp gave way to Gary Lavelle, and Gary faced only one batter, George Brett, who walked on five pitches. And then Cox went to Tom Henke.

With the Jays leading 4-3 in the ninth, Henke faced pinch hitter Pat Sheridan, a left-handed hitting outfielder for the Royals. Henke got ahead of him with two good inside fast balls. We had talked a lot about how we were going to pitch to Sheridan. We noted that he liked the ball out over the plate. Pitchers with a good fast ball could crowd him inside above the belt, and really get him out easily. Henke did that on the first two pitches and over-matched Sheridan. On the third pitch, however, he decided to go with his fork ball, and that stayed out over the plate without the velocity of the fast ball. Sheridan had the chance to get around and he hit the ball squarely, driving it into the night over the right field fence. We all had a little bit of "déja vu", as we thought back to the Wynegar home run with Henke on the mound. Once again, the score was tied 4-4 in the ninth inning.

That brought up Lonnie Smith who retired on a fly ball, and then Willie Wilson, who grounded to the right side for a single. Wilson advanced to second base on George Brett's ground out, and we were within one out of going to the bottom of the ninth with a tie ball game. Frank White was the batter, and I felt Henke could over-match him with fast balls.

Frank is a first-ball, fastball hitter who likes the ball up and out over the plate. He has a tendency to swing at balls that are out of the strike zone and up. If Henke could get his good fast-ball up a little bit above the strike zone, I was sure Frank would swing at it. The first pitch was high in the strike zone, and Frank got on top of it, driving it to centre field, a low, rocket line drive. Moseby came on charging hard. It looked as though he made the catch right at shoe level above the turf. In mass confusion, second-base umpire Ted Hendry ran out towards the play, but then hesitated because he was unsure of what to call. Moseby quickly raised his glove into the air, signifying that he had made the catch, and he continued running in, anticipating that being the third out. Wilson, who was on second and off with the crack of the bat, scored easily if the call was for a trap; if the call was for the third out, Wilson was just running in to the bench.

Hendry looked to crew chief Dave Phillips, on the right field line, and, for what seemed like an eternity, nobody made a call. Moseby kept racing in towards the infield with his glove high in the air, and his triumphant gesture of the third out. Finally, Davey Phillips ran towards centre field, signalling "safe". We couldn't believe it. The Royals had scored the run and taken the lead in Game Number Two.

Moseby obviously felt he had caught the ball (if it was a decoy, it was a very good one). He had everybody convinced, on the field at least, that he had caught it. The left-field umpire, Derryl Cousins, ran back towards centre field again signalling "safe, safe, safe", as soon as he saw Dave Phillips' signal. Ted Hendry still had not made a call and he never did make a call, out or safe, although he was the umpire who should have made the final decision.

Our bench was stunned. Garcia, Fernandez and Moseby gathered around the umpires. Phillips maintained that Moseby trapped the ball, that it hit in front of his glove, that it hit the turf before Moseby's glove, and was a trap. Phillips had a difficult angle: he was in right field on the foul line. Moseby was charging with his left hand, his glove hand, so the back of his glove faced Phillips. Davey could not really have had a very good visual shot because he was so far away.

124

This was a difficult call for him at best. Coxie came out on the field in disbelief. He was amazed — and speechless.

After the game, several of the reporters in the press box, who had studied many different angles on the replay, could not tell one way or the other whether the ball was caught or not — the play was that close!

Unfortunately, Hendry had failed to make a call. Had he made a quick call, either safe or out, I don't think anybody would have said anything; Hendry's hesitation opened the door to a lot of doubt and uncertainty.

Well, after that, we all went up and down the bench saying, "That's all right, we can score a run here, we'll tie it up — no problem." I don't know if anybody really believed it, but that's all we said.

We got things going again with Tony Fernandez leading off; he hit a ball up the middle that Concepcion, in as the defensive replacement for Biancalana, stopped back behind second base but a double clutch allowed Tony beat out at first base for a hit. The first runner was on; we only needed one run to tie it up.

Garcia followed with a swinging bunt down the third-base line moving Fernandez to second base. Now we had the tying run in position, with Moseby at the plate. The Kansas City outfielders throw average at best. Pat Sheridan, the right-fielder has the strongest arm of them all. Wilson is only fair in centre, although he makes up for it with his great speed and his ability to charge a ball; Lonnie Smith is very erratic in left field. Moseby came through with a single down the right side, and Sheridan, playing unusually deep at the time, had to charge the ball and come up throwing. Tony Fernandez got a good break off second base. Jimy Williams, the third-base coach, held up the stop sign, wanting Fernandez to hold at third, which would put runners at first and third. Fernandez ran right through. Tony felt he had gotten a good jump. He scored ahead of Sheridan's throw. The game was tied up. Moseby advanced to second base on the throw. He represented the winning run.

Kansas City ace, Dan Quisenberry, had come in on the ninth. He faced Oliver (pinch hitting for Cliff Johnson) and Bell in the tenth. I liked our chances.

Quisenberry, 31, is an unusual person, in that he's the only

125

man Kansas City looks for to save games. Dan had 37 of the 38 saves for his club and he did not come into a game unless it was a save situation. I personally don't think he was pitching as well as his record indicates. He doesn't have the velocity on his fast ball he used to have, and his submarine style needs greater velocity to help the ball sink more, making the hitters hit it on the ground. Dan does throw a few more change-ups and has tried to be trickier on the mound. Previously, he would go after batters with his good sinking ball, beating it ito the ground and utilizing the Royals' good infield defense. He doesn't seem to have that now and consequently he has a lot of difficulty with left-handed batters. Although Dan had 37 saves this year, he still gave up a lot of runs late in the ball game.

We had tied up the game, and we knew we were going to get another shot, even if we did not score. Oliver took a bad swing on the first pitch, a change-up that Quisenberry took a lot off. (Dan's submarine style is somewhat unusual, because he is the only pitcher throwing that way in the league. Batters need to make an adjustment when facing him). Oliver had faced Quisenberry many times before, but he went 2 and 0. I felt that Scoop would make contact, driving the ball somewhere to give Moseby a chance to advance at least one base.

Quisenberry set once more and delivered a fast ball to the outside part of the plate, sinking away from Oliver; Scoop went with the pitch very nicely, driving the ball past Brett at third, out of Concepcion's reach into left field. Lonnie Smith came charging hard, but Moseby had an excellent break on the ball and scored easily ahead of a feeble throw. Blue Jays 6; Kansas City 5.

We had come back and won a game that looked like anything but our game after Sheridan's home run and the controversial trap play. We had come back on a very big hit by Oliver to win the game in the tenth inning. We were in the driver's seat. The win had to be a big boost for Henke, too, because he had given up the tying run. Although I am sure he would have much rather made the save, Tom held them to get the win.

• • • •

Game Number Three of the Championship Series in Kansas City should be called the George Brett Game, no doubt about it. We had taken an early lead, scoring five runs, and we were up 5-0 with Alexander on the mound. We were feeling pretty good. I know down in the bullpen we were talking about the seven-game series, wishing we could return to the old five-game match-up, where upon this would be our third victory and we would wrap it up, getting the chance to go to the World Series. Obviously, we were very premature in counting our win.

The first pitch Brett hit off Alexander that night was a change-up. He hit it for a home run, putting the Royals on the board 5-1. We weren't concerned. Brett is a great hitter. He knew he was going to get his hits. So did we. We tipped our hats to the man and continued the game. At 5-1, our lead was comfortable.

Then Brett came up again and hit a slider inside off the right-field fence. We like to think the best way to pitch to Brett is to throw him something off-speed. He is a tremendous fast-ball hitter, and anytime he gets a fast ball, he can pretty much hit it anywhere he wants. George will hit an outside fast ball to the left; an insider he'll pull down the line. He has great discipline at the plate. George never commits himself; he doesn't over-swing. He is a very difficult man to pitch to. We still did not worry too much after giving up a double to George Brett. We knew we were going to give him some hits.

Willie Wilson singled, with the score at 5-3, bringing up Brett in the sixth inning with the chance to tie the game. Here Doyle felt that if he pitched away, pitched George on the outside half of the plate, making him use the big part of the field, the ball would stay in the ballpark. Doyle was thinking about anything other than a home run, because a home run would tie up the game. Doyle's pitch was a fast ball away, but up (a little too much) in the strike zone. George hit a fly ball to left field which looked as if it was going to be nothing more than a fly ball on the warning track. The wind kept blowing up at left and carried that ball over the fence.

George jumped about three feet off the ground at first base, and thrust his right arm high in the air. He had just tied up the game with a tremendous hitting display: a solo home run, a double, and a two-run home run — and he had hit three different pitches to three different locations in the ballpark to do it. Doyle had made three good, tough pitches. George had hit all three. It *was* George Brett Night.

• • • •

Saturday night in Kansas City, we went into the game leading the Royals in the series 2 games to 1. We won that night 3-1 with three runs at the top of the ninth, after losing 1-0 to Liebrandt for most of the night. Leibrandt was outstanding. All game long he moved his pitches in and out. I believe he had five or six balls just tapped weakly back to him on the mound, an indication that his sinker ball was working very well, and that our right-handers couldn't stay off it. His change-up, combined with his sinker ball, made him almost impenetrable.

The story changed dramatically in the ninth inning. Damaso Garcia led off and, very uncharacteristically, took four balls and walked. Garcia had had only 15 walks in 600 at-bats during the season, and I'm sure this walk Saturday night was the biggest one in his career. Leibrandt faced Moseby next.

Sometimes it seems as if Moseby is always in the middle of everything. He is a good batter, but he had been indifferent during the last two weeks of the season. He had a chance to keep the rally alive.

Lloyd took a fast ball on the inside corner of the plate and drove it deep into the right centre field alley, up against the fence. Garcia hustled around third and scored easily. The game was tied 1-1. Rick Howser came out to the mound to make a pitching change. Leibrandt's brilliant game was gone; all he could do was lose the game — it was his run at second with Moseby.

Quisenberry came in to face George Bell with nobody out. The first two pitches over-matched Bell: an inside fast ball for strike one, and an off-speed pitch on the outside for strike two. Quisenberry had Bell in the hole, but George hit the third offering with a kind of checked swing for a line drive over Frank White's head into right field. Moseby had to hold up on the pitch to make sure White couldn't catch it, and he remained at third base. There were runners at first and third, with nobody out. Cliff Johnson, the scheduled hitter, headed back to the dugout as Bobby Cox opted for Al Oliver as pinch hitter.

Al did not waste any time. He hit the first pitch down the

right field line, just inside the foul line for a base hit. Moseby scored easily, and Bell, getting a great jump on the ball, hustled around third base to beat the relay in. We took a two-run lead as Oliver stood at second base, raising a triumphant Number One into the air, acknowledging his team mates back on the bench. It had to be a devastating moment for the Royals who had been sailing along so well, although they had not hit Stieb very hard.

Al Oliver was probably the best interview on the team the next day. He even skipped batting practice because he had so many reporters around him, holding such a wonderful press conference that he could not get up and leave. Al was supposed to hit in the first group, but its time had long come and gone before he moved from the bench. Oliver knew he probably would not be with the team next year, that the Blue Jays were going with youth. He was out of his contract and probably would not be able to come back to Toronto. This series had been a great break for Al. He wanted people to know that he felt the club should sign him because he was still effective at swinging the bat and hitting the ball. Al was pretty candid about his feelings, although he wanted the press to understand that he did not want to talk about the matter at that time.

● ● ● ●

The next game, Number Five, we lost 2-0. Jim Acker was the only high spot of the day because he came in as relief and retired all eight batters he faced. Jim came in with a runner on third base and one out. Kansas City had already scored two runs, and we were down 2-0. Danny Jackson was pitching so effectively that one more run might be critical. Ack came in at that point and got Sheridan on a pop-up, Balboni on a weak ground ball and got out of the inning without an additional run given up. He held us and gave us a chance to get back into the ball game.

It must be admitted, however, that we had squandered many earlier opportunities to do so. (We had runners on second and third with nobody out, and could not score a run: two games in a row.) It was an eerie feeling. We felt that our waste of scoring opportunities earlier in the game might well come back to haunt us, particularly because Jackson had been pitching pretty much on edge all day long. He would give up a couple of hits, then dodge bullets and get out of the inning without any runs. Two or three innings in a row he did this, and we had a steadily increasing feeling that if we squandered one more opportunity, we would not be given another. Well, that's what happened. Jackson finally settled in well with his great slider, and the Blue Jays' batting machine was shut down.

Talking with Jim Sundberg after the game, I mentioned the fact that every time Jackson would get in a jam, Sunny would go out and calm him down. Sunny replied, "Yeah, you have to just put things in perspective and make sure he relaxes out there, and gets back into his good delivery and makes good pitches in this situation, because he has great stuff." Sunny said he had to play Jackson in the middle because his fast ball moves so much. "The ball moves to either side of the plate, and you do not want to get too fine with it. You want to throw it to the middle of the plate and let it work." When Jackson pitches to the corners, he loses a little bit of his velocity. When he throws for the middle of the plate, the ball's velocity takes off, and the pitch remains very effective. Jackson has one of the better sliders in the league: he throws it in a very straight, downward plane, and it always stays low in the strike zone. You can tell how good a slider is by the way the right-handed batters hit it: Blue Jay batters were swinging over the top of Jackson's pitch; it was difficult for them to lay off the ball because, coming in, it looked as if it was high enough for a strike; only at the last minute did the pitch drop down and inside.

When a batter looks out to a pitcher, he focusses above the throwing arm to that point where the ball will eventually be released. As soon as the batter can pick up the rotation, or the spin on the ball, he can determine whether it is a fast ball or a breaking ball. He can then make a judgement to determine how fast the ball is coming and at which angle it is going to break. All of the batter's decisions are made once he determines the spin on the ball. A pitcher like Jackson has such a tight spin and good velocity on his slider that one can't tell whether he is releasing a fast ball or a slider. That is what was causing the Blue Jay batters so much trouble. Jackson would throw his slider with such a tight spin that one could not even see the seams. It looked like a fast ball, but then it would come inside and break away from the hitters. This was very, very effective pitching.

Kansas City won the fifth game on two runs: one scored on an infield ground out, the second on a sacrifice fly in the second inning. That was it.

• • • •

A big thing about Game Number Six on Saturday was that we had Alexander pitching, although he was troubled somewhat by a bad leg; he had a slight hamstring pull which had happened in Kansas City on Friday. There was some strain, and Doyle was going into the game without having thrown in between. Nonetheless, if anybody could win for us that day, Doyle Alexander could. That is the kind of competitor he is.

Doyle could not help us, and the Blue Jays lost to Kansas City, 5-3. Alexander got tagged with the loss (Acker came in as relief), and Mark Gubicza got the win. Once again we stranded several players on base and had plenty of scoring chances but failed to capitalize.

After the game, Bell, who had had a couple of close calls (particularly at third base, where he was called out going from first to third, on a base hit by Cliff Johnson), was holding court with about 20 writers in front of his locker in the clubhouse. George was talking about the umpires. He was pretty emotional and was saying he thought the umpires were anti-Canadian and that they were against the Blue Jays. . . that they did not really want a Canadian series, and all that. Moseby's locker was next to Bell's. Mine was the third in that row. When Lloyd heard George talking, he said, "Hey, man, he's just kidding! He doesn't mean that, he's just kidding." George turned to him and said, "No, I'm not, I'm serious!" But, then, George is a very emotional guy.

• • • •

I don't think I've ever had a situation where I've been so nervous and uptight about a ball game as I was about the seventh game of the playoffs. I knew I could not do *anything* to help. I *wanted* to play in that game so badly. I actually felt nervous to the point of physical illness; I was a total wreck. I told Arlene several times, "I can't believe I'm this uptight, because I know I am not going to play. There is nothing I can do. My job is to try and relax everyone else, and I'm a basket-case." There was so much anxiety. I had a bad feeling about the game before it began. We had had so many opportunities to win the magical fourth game, to clinch and get into the World Series. We had let each chance slip through our hands. I kept

George Bell in front of his locker

saying to myself, "If we don't capitalize soon, we are going to run out of opportunities. Kansas City is taking advantage of every break. They're getting runners over, and driving runs in and getting the base hits when they need them."

I had a completely empty feeling when Sundberg got the bit triple and drove in three runs in the sixth inning, with two out. The score was Kansas City 5, Toronto 1. "This can't be happening to us. We've all worked so hard and now we are down to the last game." It was a nightmare. Once again in the seventh game we had bases-loaded situations and could not get a hit to produce even one run.

Frank White followed Sundberg with a base hit to make the score 6-1. The lead seemed insurmountable; we would never be able to catch the Royals.

I was down in the bullpen at that point, and made my way back to the dugout after Acker got out of the inning. I sat down next to Rance Mulliniks, who shook his head saying, "I can't believe this. This is the most disappointing thing that has ever happened to me in my life. We should be better than these guys. We *are* better than these guys. We have to score some runs . . . we have to beat these guys because we have a better ball club. . . ." He just kept shaking his head. "I can't believe this is happening." Everybody felt the same way.

Position by position I felt, and still feel, that the Blue Jays were a better team than the Royals. Ernie Whitt, behind the plate, had a better year than Sundberg did numbers-wise. At first base, I don't think Balboni, in spite of his big year with the home runs, had a sizeable advantage over Willie Upshaw, if he had any advantage at all. I feel that we had a distinct advantage at second base with Garcia (with the better average), and that we had a strong edge at shortstop with Fernandez. I had to give the advantage to Kansas City at third base; but, in left field, George Bell is a much better player overall than Lonnie Smith. Wilson is a great defensive outfielder, and he makes things happen when he gets to the plate; but I don't think he is any more of a force than Lloyd Moseby. Toronto certainly had the edge with Barfield. All well and good. In the final analysis, Kansas City executed the plays and the Blue Jays did not. It was that simple.

• • • •

I think George Bell felt he had a responsibility to carry the whole team on his shoulders: he had never been told that, he

133

had never been put in that position; but I think he took it upon himself to be the leader, to be the one that was really going to get us over the hump. I think that in so doing George got himself into some bad habits, habits which started way back in Chicago, when he had that big home run spurt. George had a great swing going then and he hit all those home runs in a row, George started swinging for home runs: his swing got longer and longer; it became a big looping swing, and George started pulling off a lot of balls.

George is a line-drive hitter who sprays the ball to all fields. He has a lot of power when he gets hold of a good ball, but he's not a Steve Balboni with a big upper-cut swing. George can't produce high, booming home runs. His home runs are line drives. They're more or less a product of a good swing. George has a good swing when he's in his groove. Pitchers in the playoff series pitched George very well. George is a low-ball hitter, and the left-handers crowded him with fast balls inside; then they turned the ball over and made it race away from George to the outside of the plate. George was hooked: he chased Leibrandt all night long. Kansas City got a good scouting report on George Bell; they stayed with him and pitched him effectively.

George wasn't swinging well either: he pulled off the ball, hitting a lot of balls on the end of the bat, reached for a lot of balls and lunged at them. He didn't keep his weight back; he moved forward with his shoulders, which caused his hands to drag through the strike zone and hit the ball on an upward plane. (A downward swing gives the batter a line drive.) George had several opportunities to break games open for us; and I think his failure to do so wasn't caused by anything more than just trying too hard.

Doyle Alexander put our loss into the proper perspective after the game (as we said our good-byes, promising to stay in touch through the next couple of months) when he said, "Y'know, we have a better team than they do, but they out-played us in this series."

• • • •

Good team, better team notwithstanding, I think we have to give Kansas City a lot of credit, particularly because they faced such adversity and triumphed. Buddy Black especially had an off year, a terrible year; he didn't pitch well until he beat the Angels on a three-hitter late in the season to clinch the Pennant. Buddy came back and gave Kansas a great game up here in Game Number Two, an outstanding game. He really had our number. We couldn't touch him. Then he hit Bell with a pitch, and his game fell apart. Leibrandt is a very good, controlled pitcher, not a Guidry, but he's a winner. He comes at you with several different pitches over the plate.

Saberhagen's 20 wins this year make him the outstanding pitcher on the Kansas City staff, and he is only 21 years old. Brett has a great feeling for pitching: he goes at hitters' weaknesses like a veteran, picking away at them and never giving in. He has a good breaking ball and he has the confidence to throw it over the plate any time in the count. Saberhagen's ability to change speeds back and forth off his fast ball, adding a little bit more, taking a little bit off, keeps the hitter off balance. It is a very important key — something you don't see in a young pitcher very often.

Danny Jackson had a great year overall. He may develop into the Number Two Kansas City pitcher. He has outstanding stuff and is very disciplined. He shut us out 2-0 in Kansas City in the playoffs. We had him on the ropes several times, but we never could produce the hit to get him out of the game; as he kept escaping from situations, his momentum kept building and building. He pitched himself out of jams all series long.

Kansas City has a lot of character, something the Blue Jays failed to acknowledge. We didn't want to talk about them as a team, although we all respected their ability. Frank White is a great second base man; Hal McRae has been a great DH (he's in the twilight of a career right now at 40), hitting 14 home runs and with 70 RBIs in about 375 at-bats. When I talked with Hal during the championship series, he said, ''They forced me to come back and play next year. They played me so much I got 70 RBIs, now I gotta come back and play next year.'' He had had thoughts of retiring but. . . . The Royals have signed Hal's son, Brian, who plays shortstop in the minor leagues for them. Hal has an outside chance of playing with his son in the major leagues, and if he plays for another couple of years, there is a possibility that Kansas might bring Brian up to play.

During the middle months of the 1985 season, every time an opposing club walked Brett, McRae hit a double. That in turn got Brett some better pitches as the months wore on. As

McRae kept producing, pitchers had to pitch better to Brett; and once again, Brett got hot. It became a cycle: McRae caused Brett to have a great year. Earlier in the year McRae was platooning with Jorge Orta, but in the middle of July, McRae became a regular. McRae definitely helped Brett hit 30 home runs and drive in 115 runs.

Jim Sundberg was another star for the Royals. We talked about him in the first meeting we had, when Bobby Cox reviewed all the opposing players. When we got to Sundberg, Moseby, who is our outfield quarterback, said, "Sundberg hits a lot of balls to right-field." We decided, "We have to pitch him inside." I took exception because I knew Sundberg had an inside-out swing, which means that he likes the ball on the inside part of the plate. He leads with his hands, and the barrel of the bat comes through behind them, causing the ball to go to the right side of the field. A pull hitter, conversely, leads with the head of his bat and pulls the ball to the left-field line. Sundberg inside-outs the ball and when he gets the ball on the inside half of the plate, that's the pitch he wants. He physically cannot inside-out a ball that's away from him. (In other words, he cannot reach for it with the head of the bat and lead with the hands at the same time.) We made mistakes on Sundberg. The first hit he got in the seventh game was a fast ball that was inside, with two strikes on him. Stieb jammed him. Although everybody on the bench said, "Oh, great pitch! We jammed him!" This was not correct: we, in fact, had made a mistake. Stieb played right into Sundberg's hands when he threw his ball inside; Sundberg fought the pitch off and hit the first run of the game.

Sundberg didn't have many hits, but they were clutches, crucial hits; and he had a big series, especially later on with the big triple, when he hit a ball that was up out over the plate, but not far enough away.

● ● ● ●

After we lost the seventh game, I sat on the bench for a long time with Jim Acker; we were watching the people run onto the field. Jim and I were both totally down in the dumps, although Jim had had a great series (he pitched only twice but pitched extremely well both times). I was gathering it all in. I think a valuable lesson was learned by all our 25 guys: *nothing* is taken for granted. We had Kansas City 3-1. We were talking about winning. We were talking about where we were going to play the World Series. . . and we forgot to make sure to go out there and play every game *to the end*. We forgot to make sure we got out there and gave our all *in every single game*. Once a series is done, you can't replay it.

I had been worried about the complacency on the team. Our young players have come up so fast, and been rewarded so quickly for not winning. I was worried that winning might be irrelevant now. Then I saw Moseby and Upshaw — two of the young leaders on the team — come into the clubhouse. Both of them had red eyes; they had obviously been crying in some backroom. I felt better because I knew that *they* knew what they had just missed: they had just missed playing in the World Series, they had missed being one of the two best teams in baseball. Everybody wants to win the World Series. Nobody remembers who lost the playoffs. After I saw Willie and Lloyd in the clubhouse, after I watched everybody going around congratulating one another on a fine year (and it had been a fine year, no matter the outcome), I realized these guys had learned a lot about themselves, and a lot about their team in 1985. I could sense a "Let me get this thing started again. — Let's think about next year. — What do we have to do to get over the top? — We're a better team than they are, but we didn't show it. — We have to show it every time we go out there!" — feeling; and it was very satisfying.

I went down to the lounge. Stieb had showered and changed into his street clothes some time before. He was sitting in the lounge, sipping on a beer and really looking down. I have never seen Dave Stieb like that before. I've seen him upset; I've seen him mad that the team hadn't performed well; mad that he had made a bad pitch; but this time he was really down. I said, "Hey, you gave us three grand efforts in a seven-game series. You pitched your heart out for us."

"This really hurts," he replied, and lapsed into silence.

Later, as I was talking to Acker and Caudill, all three of us agreed that the 1985 loss may well make Dave Stieb the pitcher that he really should be. Dave knows what it's all about now. You can't really achieve anything until you win as a team. If we had to pay the price of losing, the reward of seeing young men realize and put into proper perspective what winning *really* means may have made our loss a worthwhile experience. The Blue Jays team has the capability to win one, two, three, four, five years in a row. Maybe our 1985 loss set us on the right track.

● ● ● ●

It was a disappointed clubhouse and it was a relieved clubhouse. It was also a unified, and a warm clubhouse. A bunch of us gathered in the trainers' room and chuckled over a fan's comments: "Well, we had a wonderful summer. It was a great year for the city, and a great year for the Blue Jays and we're proud of them all!"

CHAPTER 13

Bobby Cox and Jimy Williams

WHEN BOBBY COX JOINED THE BLUE JAYS IN 1982, WE REALLY did not know an awful lot about him. He didn't know an awful lot about us. He was up front about that fact in his very first meeting with us at spring training. Bobby wanted to analyse everybody, to take a good look, and to confer with the other coaches to see how they felt (the hold-over coaches were Al Widmar and Jimy Williams). That first spring training was a learning experience for all of us. The players had to learn what Coxie expected from them.

Right off the bat we could see that Bobby communicated well, and that he was a very hard worker. He would throw batting practice, and hit fly balls and ground balls to the fielders: he enjoyed being on the field. Bobby was not that far removed from being a player himself (His last playing days were in 1970 at Syracuse, part of the Yankee system. His last major league play was in 1969 with the Yankees.) Bobby could relate to young players, and we had an abundance of them on the Blue Jay staff.

Spring training was a tough time for Bobby, but he made the cuts, and, when he got down to his final team, and broke camp for that first year's opening day, Coxie established a practice I had never seen before. Bobby talked individually with each player before our first game: he told each man

A dejected Bobby Cox after Toronto lost Game Number Seven of the American League Championship Series to Kansas City

what was expected, what each player's job would be, and what his role would be on the club. Bobby gained instant credibility with that move. He made sure all through the season that every player always knew what to expect. Bobby was always available to talk if you did not agree with something: he would discuss the matter with you and explain his thinking. He was very frank.

The Blue Jays won only 78 games in 1982, but everyone could sense a dramatic change. Cox had tremendous intensity; he had one thing on his mind — to get his ball club to a winning posture as quickly as possible. We improved dramatically in 1983, winning 89 games.

Cox introduced the platoon structure, and we platooned in several positions: behind the plate, a third base, and in right and left fields. No one on the team ever felt he was an "extra" man. We always felt all 15 players would be utilized at one point or another. Bobby made sure no one went more than a week without playing, getting up to bat, or appearing in the field defensively. He kept everybody sharp, everybody feeling a part of the team. He knew, as a former player, that that feeling was important.

One aspect of Bobby's dedication to the ball club was the fact that he regularly arrived at the stadium at one o'clock in the afternoon whenever he had a night game. Coxie would talk with the visiting coaches about other clubs the Blue Jays were scheduled to play in the future, hoping he might get some recent and inside information on batters, pitchers, and any other factors which might affect a win. Bobby never missed a trick: he had tremendous skill in evaluating talent. Coxie saw the spark in Doyle Alexander, in Davie Collins, in Fred McGriff, and many others. His pitching judgement was good, and he had good in and out movements during games. Once in a while, Bobby may have placed too much confidence in his starters, but this may well have been the result of not having a quality bullpen. After the Blue Jays built up their pitching staff in 1985, Bobby went to his relievers as quickly as any manager: his bullpen led the American league in saves this year.

Bobby Cox was a predictable manager, especially with the talent in the field. He platooned a lot, and did not bunt much. Other teams knew that if they made a pitching change, Bobby would counter with his platoon players. He stuck by

Jimy Williams

his rules through thick and thin, hot streaks and slumps. Bobby's predictability gave his players a lot of confidence because we knew what to expect, always. Bobby did not waiver. When I had my batting slump in early '85, Coxie stuck by me. "This is the man I have confidence in. He is going to play against the left-handed pitchers, and he is going to be my catcher when there is a left-hander starting." That was that.

When Bobby felt a player was not giving the team his best shot, he would have a talk with that player immediately, privately, and clear the air. He'd say, "Listen, this is not the way I want things done: I want you to do this my way. That is the way it will be done around here." Bobby would say whatever had to be said, and then forget it. He did not hold grudges. Bobby never criticized his players openly to the media either. He backed his people all the way. When something went wrong, and a player made a bad play, or pitch, Coxie would announce, "In his judgement it was the right thing to do. I'll stand behind his judgement." Bobby might talk to a player later about the selection of pitches, or the judgement used in a defensive play, but that was a private talk. Bobby felt that the players were responsible for the Blue Jays' success: he never took credit for the team.

Coxie was a great person to talk to when you needed a wise and friendly ear. A couple of times when my wife was sick at home I had to tell him, "I think I'm going to have to go home for a day and help out." He never hesitated. "You have to go with your family. Your family is Number 1! Make sure you take care of them."

Bobby's forward-looking attitude, and his responsibility as a father and husband were a very good example to the rest of the players. Every time he had an opportunity to go home and be with his family on an off day (even if it involved flying across the country at night), Bobby went. We knew he had tremendous dedication to, and love for his family.

I think all 25 Blue Jays feel very proud to have played under Bobby Cox for four years. I knew we are all happy for him, and wish him well in Atlanta. Bobby taught us how to win. He taught us what it takes to win. The Blue Jays now have a firm foundation beneath them, and Bobby Cox deserves a lot of credit for that base.

Jimy Williams, the new Blue Jays' manager, has been with

Bobby Cox

Bobby Cox and John Sullivan arguing a close call

the club since 1979. He spent seven years with the California Angels' minor league system prior to that. Jimy was the Third Base Coach and Assistant Manager under Bobby Cox. He was responsible for defensive alignments, and the infielders' work (particularly on defense) during games. Jimy moved the infielders around in response to different hitters' abilities. He was a very active Third Base Coach, and he worked hard.

Jimy communicates very well with the players: he is an upbeat guy and a fun guy to have around. He has done a great job with some of the infielders: Fernandez and Garcia, Iorg and Mulliniks. Jimy himself was an infielder. His youth relates well to the ball team. He knows the types of players we have, and what it takes for those players to perform well day in and day out.

I think Jimy Williams will be a good manager. He is very much a student of the game. He prepares himself well: he has good knowledge of the opposition and their defensive and offensive potential. He is also a good judge of outfielders' arms, of his own team's speed, and his team's abilities on the bases.

Jimy was one of the more popular coaches, and this on as good a coaching staff as I have ever been associated with. All the Blue Jay coaches are hard workers: they are all dedicated to the team. They prepare themselves well, and they are always readily available to players to talk about the game, to help with strategies or mechanical problems, or whatever.

Jimy Williams has a good accurate knowledge of pitchers and their abilities. Jimy will study every pitch in a ball game, trying to discover why a pitcher does certain things, and what might be a good, effective pitch in any given situation. He knows a manager may be only as strong as his Pitching Coach — or, in fact, only as strong as his Pitching, Batting, First Base, Third Base, and Bullpen Coaches.

Jimy Williams is a strong team player. He is a fitting successor to Bobby Cox, and I feel sure he will lead our ball club to victory for many years.

CHAPTER 14

Martinez on Martinez

IN 1981, I WAS A MEMBER OF THE MILWAUKEE BREWERS. I HAD played with Milwaukee for three years and had platooned, basically playing every other day, sharing the catching duties with Charlie Moore. During the winter of '80 the Brewers made a big trade with the St. Louis Cardinals and picked up Ted Simmons, who they intended to play as the regular catcher. Moore and myself were destined for a back-up role, at least, and, we hoped, an opportunity to be traded. As spring training progressed, Harry Dalton, the Brewers' general manager, promised me several times that I would be traded and that Milwaukee would try to accommodate my wish of going to a team where I'd have the opportunity to play. Late March arrived, then early April. I could see that nothing was in the wind; there was no longer even talk of a trade. I didn't play at all during the spring training games.

When we opened up the season, I was the fourth-string catcher on a team that was going to use only one. Charlie Moore, Ned Yost, a young catcher from the minor league system, and myself were all going to back up Simmons. It seemed that an abundance of talent was being wasted and that the Brewers could use the spots on the roster much more effectively with other players. April passed. I still hadn't played; I never left the bullpen, where I was a bullpen catcher. I never approached the plate as a pinch hitter and never played a game. Finally Buck Rogers, who is now the Montreal Expos manager, called me into the office after batting practice in Anaheim before a game against the Angels. Paul Molitor had been injured during the game the night before, and Milwaukee needed to make a quick move to get an infielder up. They also needed an additional pitcher on the roster, and my time had come. I was put on the designated "move" list, which meant that they didn't know what to do with me, but they had to free up a spot on the roster. The designated move status lasts for ten days — and it's really a limbo period. I called Arlene back at the hotel in Anaheim and told her what had happened, and that we'd pack up and go north to Sacramento, where my folks were, to gather our thoughts.

I had a lot of mixed feelings about possibly being out of baseball during that period. I felt I still had ability and talent and I was surprised that no one had tried to get me, to make a deal for me. Later I found out several teams, including the Yankees, wanted to trade for me, but the Brewers were simply asking too much.

On the ninth day of that ten-day period (I would become a free agent after ten days, and really be out in the cold), I went out bike riding, trying to stay in shape. When I came back, there was a bottle of champagne on the table. My mother and Arlene were both smiling from ear to ear. I figured something had happened. They told me that I had been traded to the Toronto Blue Jays. We all were very relieved. I was going to go to Toronto. Later as I talked with some of the players who had kept in touch with me, they expressed concern about my new club. A few even said, "I feel sorry for you, going to Toronto." I felt they were crazy or misinformed.

Roy Howell had played in Toronto under the Bavasi Regime and he was miserable. He said everything was a situation of "lord and worker"; the ballplayers and the front office were miles apart, and there was no communication between them. The earlier players, I was told, were simply hired to work and were not to concern themselves with anything else. Everyone complained about the ballpark, about Toronto, about having to go through customs all the time, about unfriendly Canadians, about the fans who weren't

147

very knowledgeable and so on. It sounded to me like an awful lot of idle griping.

When we came to Toronto, Arlene and I found that some of the players resented the fact that I was joining the team. We were the newcomers and I had replaced a catcher named Dan Whitmer. Some people took personal offence at the fact that I was taking Whitmer's job. I thought this was unusual, because most veteran ball clubs accepted change: the fact that new people would come and go.

Ernie Whitt welcomed me. He knew we were both battling for the same job, but I don't think there was any resentment. I think he felt that my coming was probably a move to help the ball club. He had enough sense at that time to realize that the team had to make some changes, had to make some steps forward, if they were going to ever become successful. The Blue Jays were going to have to make some deals.

I was excited about the city; I was glad to be part of it and, most of all, I was excited about being able to play again. I was a good Blue Jay promoter because, quite simply, I was happy to be a Blue Jay. I didn't care whether we played in the Arctic Circle, I was happy to be playing once again.

Arlene and I found a place to stay on the Lakeshore (where we've stayed almost every baseball season since), and the Blue Jay Club presented us with a car. I heard players saying, "Yeah, but it's a Honda!" I couldn't believe it! We didn't have to bring our own cars to Toronto, trekking them across the border, fighting with customs, etc. I thought it a very welcome and thoughtful move on the part of Blue Jay management, and I was upset with the players' attitude. It seemed that they were trying to make excuses to be miserable when, in fact, the only reason they were feeling bad was because we had a bad ball team. There were constant complaints; but I did not see much of a team effort to improve, either individually as players, or collectively.

● ● ● ●

When I came to Toronto in 1981, Bobby Mattick was the manager, Peter Bavasi was the general manager. We had a players' strike and we had a bad team. We all knew Danny Ainge was on the verge of playing basketball; he signed with the Boston Celtics, where he is still playing. Many players were borderline major leaguers; they were expansion players who would eventually be weeded out as the team got more and more competitive. Ken Macha was on the team and, although he probably deserved a better opportunity, he eventually went to Japan where he's still playing baseball. Rick Bosetti thought he was being held down in Toronto, demanded to be traded, to go somewhere else where he could become an everyday player. When he did get traded, Rick became a reserve player and, within a year or two, he was totally out of the game. Jerry Garvin, who was an original Blue Jay, has left baseball.

Probably the most significant change for the Blue Jays was the appointment of Pat Gillick as general manager. Simultaneously, Peter Hardy moved into an active role with the ball club, as the chief executive officer. Gillick then made the move to bring in Bobby Cox, who had been fired by Atlanta. Each of these moves signalled the Blue Jays drive to improve. We had hit rock-bottom; we were cellar-dwellers from the first year we arrived in the league. It was time to make a change. Some of the early players had reached a point where they became competitive; they began to show promise. The team grew better and better each year.

● ● ● ●

Overall, I think my coming to Toronto has been the biggest break of my career. It's funny how playing good baseball makes you realize other things aren't that important.

We American players make certain adjustments when we come across the border; but I don't think there's any city in North America that can compare with Toronto, as far as its cleanliness, its safety, the reliability of the police force, the transportation, the ease getting around the city, the highways, the nightlife and the restaurants. To me, Toronto is a polished New York.

I must say, though, the Canadian tax structure is exactly the reason why American ballplayers don't live here year round. Most Americans rely on their ability to write off the mortgage interest on their house as a tax benefit. You can't do that in Canada, and the lack of a mortgage-interest deduction is the Number One disadvantage to living here. Personally, I think a Dave Stieb, or a Lloyd Moseby, or a Jesse Barfield available year round, to promote the Blue Jays and himself, would be enormously beneficial to Toronto. There is a huge market for endorsements and public-speaking engagements. I would come and live up here in a minute if I was 27 or 28 years old, knowing that I was going to play here for a few more years. Even with my career headed in the direction it is, with broadcasting as a possibility in the off season, I should probably be living here now. It's a logical place for me to be, but I just haven't made the move.

• • • •

Before I began my career as a professional baseball player, I went to college where I took accounting. Like anyone else aged 17 or 18 who must decide what education he/she should have, I was poorly prepared. I thought accounting would be good for me. Most of my friends were in physical education, and I did not want to be part of that physical education "jock" syndrome. I didn't want to be stereotyped. "Well, you're playing baseball, you must be in physical education." I did not want to do that, but I still feel I wasted my college years because my mind was always on professional baseball. My future was professional baseball, and I felt I would play baseball all my life.

Young players, particularly players like Manny Lee, Lloyd Moseby, or Dave Stieb, who come into the game at 24-25, see no end in sight. Baseball goes on forever in their minds. That was certainly how I felt. I didn't really think about the end of my career; I never thought about a career-ending injury. You tend not to plan ahead, and over and over, I've seen what lack of planning has done to players I've played with. They never thought about the fact that the average major league career lasts only four years.

Young players do know that the opportunity to play baseball is a year round process. They take better care of themselves; they are more aware of physical training in the off season. And, some are able and do play until 44-45 years of age because the money is there to be made.

Baseball players who have performed well, can be rewarded to the tune of a million dollars a year. They need solid financial advice because, for the most part, they don't know enough themselves to manage their money successfully. We want to believe our player's agents are competent, very loyal to their players, and always do a good job. Such is not always the case, however. I am involved with the player's union. We are concerned about players and their post-baseball lives: we want to make sure there are no wasted opportunities. We monitor players' agents, and we evaluate and approve them so players, when they do hire an agent, know that he/she is genuine, with a solid background, and has the player's best interests at heart.

Good financial advice should allow a baseball player to retain his lifestyle after his baseball career is over. The flat, raw expenses of any baseball player are high: two or three households (the base home, the residence in the team's home city, and the spring training residence for 6-8 weeks). When I started out playing in the major leagues, the minimum salary was $10,000. It was not until 1976 that salaries increased to a level where players did not have to work through the winter to earn supplemental income. Earlier in my career, all baseball players regularly went to winter ball.

In 1975, the highest paid player in Kansas City was making $80,000. In Toronto in 1985, the minimum salary is $60,000. A dramatic difference.

I did not start my financial planning until 3-4 years ago. I never made enough money to worry about the future. I was just getting by from year to year, hoping that the next year I would still have a job to continue my lifestyle.

I met my financial people on a hunting trip: I had hunted with this fellow for 3 or 4 years, and never really knew what he did. One day, though, we got to talking about his job. He told me he was a certified financial planner, and I said, "Well, that's kind of interesting. I'd like to talk to you sometime, about my finances and everything." We talked.

I discovered from him how basically backwards baseball players' finances were. He learned from me that ball clubs like their players to be financially naive, because it keeps the players dependent on the club. Good financial background and good financial planning make a player independent, and therefore less reliant on the club. Players less dependent on the club are able to make more demands because they have more financial security.

● ● ● ●

I don't think the large baseball salaries result in an excessive amount of flashiness on the part of players' lifestyles. Everyone likes the idea of fancy cars and nice suits, but basically, most of the players live and play baseball: they don't have time for "rich and famous" living. The fundamental backgrounds of the Blue Jays' players, in particular, are very solid. We are not going to change personalities simply because we

Arlene, Casey and me

have some additional dollars in our pockets. Our lifestyles do not seem to be extravagant, either during the season, or after it is over.

Lloyd Moseby goes fishing on the American River, outside Sacramento during the off season. Jimmy Acker will be back in Freer, Texas, (where he has lived all his life) working in the restaurant/motel his family owns, making coffee and serving customers. Jimmy does a lot of deer hunting in the off season, and he has a brand new house which his sister is decorating for him. Dave Stieb goes home to Florida, plays golf, goes fishing, and enjoys his family. There is a cruise that a sporting company puts on for people once in a while, and Dave will probably go on that. Doyle Alexander will be working on building his new home in Arlington, Texas. Doyle, too, will be hunting and fishing, and playing racquetball to stay in shape. He will stick close to home because his daughter is in high school, and his son in elementary school. Doyle will probably hunt a lot of deer with Danny Darwin, who pitches for the Brewers. Ernie Whitt will probably also go hunting. Ernie lives in Detroit, and he has just signed up with Labatt's. I'm sure there will be promotional appearances planned for Ernie in Toronto this winter.

Damaso Garcia will ship his Mercedes down to the Dominican Republic, and probably stick pretty close to home.

• • • •

Garcia, Bell and Fernandez are on the verge of being national heroes in their own country. Baseball is very important to the Dominican Republic because it gives many young players the opportunity to make a good living. Many older Dominican players have done very well at home, after their baseball career is over. Not one of the Dominican players on the Blue Jays' team grew up in wealthy circumstances; now that they are making money, each one of them is taking care of his family first. Manny Lee is building a home for his parents, and he is only 19 years old!

• • • •

As soon as I get home, right after the World Series, I will start going to rehab daily. I will be lifting weights, and, hopefully, my ankle will come around to a point where I can do ropes again.

Arlene and I will go to Hawaii for the Players' Association

meetings in December; in January we'll take a cruise to the Caribbean on the Princess line, and in February we'll go to Scottsdale, Arizona to play in the American Airlines' Golf Tournament. My family spends a lot of time together in the off season. I'll be home with Casey, who will be playing basketball this winter in his first organized sports endeavour. He's looking forward to it and I'm looking forward to helping him.

• • • •

I have a difficult time adjusting to the American pursuit of excellence in sports for children. I'm really upset when I see 4-5-year-old kids playing soccer, running in sprints, doing push-ups, and crying their hearts out when they lose a game. We have held Casey out of organized sports for this reason. We want him to develop in other areas first: musically (he has talent), and academically. We want Casey to understand that a game is a game, and no more than a game (ability and talent may allow one to earn a living from sport, but that comes later). Casey loves baseball; he likes hockey and basketball. He loves sports. He plays for fun and he enjoys it. That is important.

• • • •

I will be thinking about spring training the moment the World Series is over. I'm 37 years old, going into my 18th spring training, and I was injured in the 1985 season: I have a *lot* of work to do. This is a challenge I am excited about. I will work hard. There will be pain, and frustration, but I will make it through. I want to play again. I know I *can* play again, and not for just one more year. I will be in Florida on February 15, two weeks early for spring training, and I will be ready to play at that time. There is no doubt whatsoever in my mind.

Spring training is a good time for Arlene, Casey and myself. It is a vacation, with a little bit of baseball thrown in. Arlene spends the time on the beach, Sand Key, just south of Clearwater, where we have a condominium. Casey has a tutor three times a week and does all his schoolwork (he is usually ahead of his classmates when we return to Kansas as a result of that intense one-on-one learning experience). We fish, go dancing, limber up, run, and play some baseball!

154

I feel that the 1985 season, when the Blue Jays won 99 games and went down to the last weekend of the series before we clinched the pennant was a grand season for us in every respect. It was certainly a very rewarding season.

Some of the players' performances may not have been what they were in 1983 and 1984, but others took up the slack successfully. Ernie Whitt had his best year ever. Moseby and Upshaw both had off years. They struggled through the first half of the season, although Willie got off to a better start than Lloyd. By mid-season, their performances were noticeably short of their ability. They both struggled with average, with power, and with run production.

I remember when Willie ordered a new bat to arrive for the Texas series. He had always done well in Texas in the presence of his family, all of whom attended the Rangers' games. Willie's new bat was Model 064, an unusual model with a very thin handle. Willie had tested Al Oliver's bat before Oliver was a team mate of ours. Willie's earlier bat was a very basic one, the P72, which is used by several players including Mulliniks, Iorg, Upshaw and Moseby. Willie's drastic change to a very thin handled 'radical" bat resulted in a home run, and he felt, "Yes, this is my answer — big change. . . ." As that bat logged more and more at-bats, Willie began to over-swing. He is not a pull hitter, but rather a spray hitter who utilizes all parts of the field. Willie's over-confidence with his new bat started to cause him problems. He pulled off the bat, started over-swinging and forcing things, obviously thinking, "If I swing real hard, I'll get a hit, hit the ball harder." Actually, when you over-swing, you move away from the ball. I think Willie stuck with his new bat too long and hit a real slump.

Finally, he made a bat change, and went back to the P72. Hits started to come. Willie began to hit the ball to left-centre, to right-centre; and he was getting the big clutch hits. His average rose: .250, .260 and finally .275, not a bad year — particularly when he had been at .230 for the greater part of the season. Willie had 65 RBIs in 1985 compared to a career high of 104 in '83.

Moseby has a very confident, aggressive swing. He swings so hard sometimes that he pulls himself off the ball. He really hit that groove this year. I think he was too tentative at the

155

plate for most of the year, never comfortable, never in a frame of mind where he thought he could hit everything. Lloyd is a very successful hitter when he's patient, when he looks for the ball out over the plate, driving it where it is pitched. He is not that different from Mulliniks, Brett, Boggs or any of the great hitters, all of whom stayed within themselves striving to hit the ball where it's pitched. There are very few batters who can pull the ball all the time successfully.

Moseby's average rose in August and September to .259 for the season, 40 points down from where he should have been. Bobby Cox and Cito Gaston talked a lot with Lloyd about how he had changed his style. Lloyd had made a very, very subtle adjustment with his hands, lowering them a little, so they were not in the same spot they had been in '83 and '84. Lloyd did not believe he had made that change. He felt comfortable; he felt he was in the same spot. It became a matter of pride. "I'm all right, I'm comfortable, I can hit from here; don't worry about me; I'll get out of it." Moseby's youthful ego got involved to the point where he didn't want to make a re-adjustment. He didn't really know whether his stance was right or wrong. He felt he could work it out himself, and he did have the ability to work it out in time. All players need some help at times. If Lloyd had been more receptive to suggestions, possibly making a little adjustment, perhaps he would have gotten into a better groove earlier in 1985.

George Bell had 95 RBIs, and Jesse Barfield was a major force with 27 home runs and 88 RBIs. Tony Fernandez proved he was an everyday player, hitting .289 (which surprised everybody, I think, because we've always thought of Tony more as a wizard at defense). Garcia had another steady year, and the pitching staff was outstanding, as the team lead the league in ERA. The bullpen saved more games than any other in the American league. We had solid strength with Henke, Caudill, Acker, Lavelle, and Dennis Lamp.

● ● ● ●

Nevertheless, by next spring, I am sure there will be several new faces in camp. Starting another campaign will be just as exciting as starting in 1985. Pat Gillick and Jimy Williams have already started to evaluate the team, to ascertain what areas need to be improved upon, and where changes need to be made. Standing still, in this game, is deadly.

I think management will be looking at the DH. Cliff Johnson came back and gave us a good solid month and a half, and Al Oliver contributed a lot after he joined us in July, but I don't know if Gillick and Williams want to commit to either player as a full time DH next year. I think Cecil Fielder is going to have a very good lookover in spring training. And there will be all those possibilities of going outside the organization. I have heard talk of Donny Baylor, of Dave Winfield, and Gorman Thomas in Seattle — all proven hitters with a lot of power. I am sure Gillick will listen to all options.

Naturally, there will be talk about improving the bench. We had two guys, Thornton and Lee, who were basically unavailable to help us. They had been put on the team simply because they were drafted and had to be protected by inclusion on the major league roster. I think Gillick and Williams both feel we need to shore up the bench, and that Rick Leach is a very good candidate for filling that role.

I think the team realizes we need to have some catching help, no matter whether I come back 100% in 1986 or not. Ernie Whitt was obviously worn down at the end of the season. Although Jeff Hearron did not play a great deal in 1985, I think he needs to sharpen his skills again in the minor leagues before coming back to Toronto. We saw that shopping around for catchers in the middle of the season was not a good practice because there is not generally a lot of talent available at that time. Everybody knows that good catching is difficult to find.

The Blue Jays have always talked about replacing me; each year they talk, and every spring, they talk about replacing me because I'm getting old, and they don't know how much longer I can play. I am not concerned. I think of talk like that as a challenge. I don't feel I have to show anybody anything. I go out there and play. I will make sure I do my homework so I am ready to play in 1986. Anyone looking to take over my catching position with the Blue Jays next year will have one hell of a fight for the job.

Although the pitching staff seems secure, the pitchers themselves have a lot of doubt about their roles in 1986. Obviously we know that Stieb, Alexander, Key and Clancy will probably be back. Dennis Lamp is, I feel, very secure, and Tom Henke as well. Jimmy Acker thinks he is going to move on; Billy Caudill thinks the same, and Gary Lavelle has some arm trouble (although I think he will be able to get over that in the wintertime.) Then there is John Cerutti, and Tom Filer, who was 7 and 0 for us. They are going to fit in.

I think Steve Davis is a very good possibility as a left-handed starter. He came up and threw some good games for us. Management will not make a move simply to get a left-handed starter, however, if the quality is not there. Steve will have to work hard to get the job. Even Luis Leal, who was sent off to the minor leagues, may be back. (Luis, however, might well be traded because he was not called back in September).

There are undoubtedly several young guys we don't even know about yet, who will show up in spring training, with impressive arms, coming off fine winter ball seasons.

Silvestre Campusano will probably also be at spring training. His name is being bantered around quite a bit now. Campusano is from the Dominican Republic, from George Bell's home team, and he is an 18 year old outfielder. He has a lot of ability. Some people suggest that Silvestre is much like the young Roberto Clemente. He is not very big, but he does do everything well: runs, hits with power, and has a great throwing arm. I personally don't think he is quite ready for the major leagues, but I have never seen him play. I am certain he will be at spring training, and the subject of very close evaluation.

A lot of teams now realize that the Blue Jays have talent, maybe even a surplus of talent. I think many people are going to come knocking on the Blue Jays' door this winter. It would not surprise me at all to find a lineup on Pat Gillick's doorstep this very morning.

THE 1985 TORONTO BLUE JAYS

Box 7777, Adelaide Street Post Office
Toronto, Ontario M5C 2K7
(416) 595-0077

CLUB DIRECTORY

BOARD OF DIRECTORS
John Craig Eaton, William Ferguson, L.G. Greenwood,
N.E. Hardy, R. Howard Webster, P.N.T. Widdrington

OFFICERS
Chairman of the Board   R. Howard Webster
Vice-Chairman, Chief Executive Officer   N.E. Hardy
Executive Vice-President, Business   Paul Beeston
Executive Vice-President, Baseball   Pat Gillick
Vice-President, Baseball   Al LaMacchia
Vice-President, Baseball   Bob Mattick
Vice-President, Finance   Bob Nicholson

FRONT OFFICE
Director, Public Relations   Howard Starkman
Director, Operations   Ken Erskine
Director, Ticket Operations   George Holm
Director, Marketing   Paul Markle
Director, Group Sales   Maureen Haffey
Director, Canadian Scouting   Bob Prentice
Administrator, Player Personnel   Gord Ash
Assistant Administrator, Player Personnel   Carolyn Thiers
Manager, Promotions   Colleen Burns
Assistant Director, Public Relations   Gary Oswald
Assistant Director, Ticket Operations   Len Frejlich
Manager, Accounting   Phil Martin
Manager, Employee Compensation   Catherine Elwood
Finance Assistant   Sue Sostarich
Trainer & Director Team Travel   Ken Carson
Director, Security   Fred Wootton
Co-ordinator, Group Sales   John MacLachlan
Manager, Ticket Vault   Paul Goodyear
Manager, Ticket Mail Services   Randy Low
Manager, Ticket Revenue   Mike Maunder
Manager, Commerce Court   Leslie Logan
Manager, Operations   Rick Amos
Supervisor, Maintenance   Dave Hamilton
Supervisor, Grounds   Brad Bujold
Supervisor, Security   Bob Sharpe
Supervisor, Office Services   Mark Graham
Team Physician   Dr. Ron Taylor
Consulting Orthopedic Surgeon   Dr. Allan Gross
Consulting Physician (Dunedin)   Dr. Martin Kornreich
Equipment Manager   Jeff Ross
Visiting Clubhouse   Ian Duff

ADMINISTRATIVE PERSONNEL
Accounting   Lori-Ann Wills
Business Operations   Sue Cannell
Group Sales   Betty Ann Armstrong
Marketing   Janet Donaldson
Operations   Pam Crepinsek
Player Personnel   Sue Turjanica, Ellen Harrigan, Sue Allen
Public Relations   Judy Van Zutphen, Debbie Alleyne
Receptionist/Switchboard   June Sym, Cindy Holden,
   Anne Jarvis
Ticket Department   Fran Brown, Allan Koyanagi, Helen
   Maunder, Frank Padget, Al Ross, Sheila Cantarutti,
   Barb Walker

BLUE JAYS PLAYER DEVELOPMENT
Executive Vice-President, Baseball   Pat Gillick
Vice-President, Baseball   Bob Mattick
Vice-President, Baseball   Al LaMacchia
Administrator, Player Personnel   Gord Ash
Assistant Administrator, Player Personnel   Carolyn Thiers
Director, Canadian Scouting   Bob Prentice
Minor League Hitting Instructor   John Mayberry
Minor League Catching Instructor   Joe Lonnett
Administrative Assistant   Susan Turjanica
Secretary, Player Personnel   Ellen Harrigan
Secretary, Player Personnel   Sue Allen·

SCOUTING SUPERVISORS
Des Plaines, IL   Chris Bourjos
Marianna, FL   Ellis Dungan
Manheim, PA   Bob Engle, Eastern Regional Scouting
   Director
Yukon, OK   Joe Ford
Santo Domingo, DR   Epy Guerrero
McKinney, TX   Jim Hughes
Arvado, CO   Moose Johnson, Special Assignment Scout
Charlotte, NC   Duane Larson
Upland, CA   Larry Maxie
Long Beach, CA   Steve Minor
Morgan Hill, CA   Wayne Morgan, Western Regional
   Scouting Director
Hershey, PA   Ben McLure
Scarborough, ONT   Bob Prentice
Pittsfield, MA   Paul Ricciarini
Berrien Springs, MI   Don Welke
Dunedin, FL   Tim Wilken
Orlando, FL   Dave Yoakum

1985 ATTENDANCE: The Blue Jays set an all-time attendance record in 1985 of 4,311,035 (3,819,181, 1984) while
setting club marks at home 2,468,925 (2nd in American
League) (2,110,009, 1984) and on the road 1,842,110 (4th in
American League).

160

TORONTO BLUE JAYS 1985 PLAYER TRANSACTIONS

DATE	PLAYER	TRANSACTION
Mar. 25	Jim Clancy - P	Placed on 21-day Disabled List (appendectomy).
Apr. 7	Ron Shepherd - OF	Placed on 15-day Disabled List (right elbow).
Apr. 21	Jim Clancy - P	Sent to Knoxville (AA) on medical rehabilitation.
Apr. 22	Ron Shepherd - OF	Activated.
Apr. 30	Willie Aikens - DH	Designated for Assignment.
	Jim Clancy - P	Recalled from medical rehabilitation at Knoxville (AA) and reinstated from 21-day Disabled List.
May 15	Willie Aikens - DH	Released outright.
July 5	Luis Leal - P	Optioned to Syracuse (AAA).
July 6	Tom Filer - P	Purchased from Syracuse (AAA).
July 9	Len Matuszek - DH - 1B	Traded to Los Angeles Dodgers in exchange for Al Oliver - DH.
July 10	Buck Martinez - C	Placed on 21-day Disabled List (dislocated right ankle and broken right fibula).
	Gary Allenson - C	Purchased from Syracuse (AAA).
July 18	Ron Shepherd - OF	Designated for Assignment.
	Cecil Fielder - 1B - DH	Purchased from Knoxville (AA).
July 25	Ron Shepherd - OF	Outrighted to Syracuse (AAA).
July 27	Jim Clancy - P	Placed on 15-day Disabled List (tendinitis-right shoulder).
July 28	Tom Henke - P	Purchased from Syracuse (AAA).

Aug. 24	Gary Allenson - C	Released outright.
	Ron Musselman -P	Optioned to Syracuse (AAA).
	Steve Davis - P	Purchased from Syracuse (AAA).
	Jeff Hearron - C	Purchased from Knoxville (AA).
Aug. 28	Jim Clancy - P	Moved to 21-day Disabled List.
	Tom Filer - P	Placed on 15-day Disabled (tender right elbow).
Aug. 29	Cliff Johnson - DH	Acquired from Texas Rangers for Matt Williams - P, Jeff Mays - P and a player to be named later.
Sept. 1	Kelly Gruber - IF	Recalled from Syracuse (AAA).
	John Cerutti - P	
	Rick Leach - OF	Purchased from Syracuse (AAA)
	Ron Shepherd - OF	
	Steve Nicosia - C	Signed as a Free Agent.
Sept. 2	Jim Clancy - P	Activated from Disabled List.
Sept. 7	Stan Clarke - P	Recalled from Syracuse (AAA).

1985 TORONTO BLUE JAYS HIGHS & LOWS

TEAM BATTING

Most Runs, Game, Blue Jays.	13, September 24, Milwaukee (A)
Most Runs, Game, Opponents	13, September 18, Boston (A)
Most Runs, Inning, Blue Jays	6, April 13, Baltimore (A), 4th inning
	6, April 24, Kansas City (H), 3rd inning
	6, May 7, Oakland (H), 6th inning
	6, June 25, Milwaukee (H), 3rd inning
	6, September 15, New York (A), 3rd inning
Most Runs, Inning, ... Opponents	6, April 13, Baltimore (A), 8th inning
	6, May 15, California (H), 9th inning
	6, September 12, New York (A), 7th inning
Most Hits, Game, Blue Jays .	22, September 29, Milwaukee (A)
Most Hits, Game, Opponents	18, April 27, Texas (A), 10 innings
	18, September 18, Boston (A), 9 innings

Most Hits, Inning, Blue Jays .	7, August 13, Baltimore (A), 4th inning
	7, September 15, New York (A), 3rd inning
	7, September 29, Milwaukee (A)
Most Hits, Inning, Opponents	7, July 20, Oakland (H), 2nd inning
Most Home Runs, Game, Blue Jays	** 5, July 10, Seattle (A)
Most Home Runs, Game, Opponents	4, May 29, Chicago (A)
Most Home Runs, Inning, Blue Jays	2, 16 times
Most Home Runs, Inning, Opponents	3, 9th inning, August 24, Chicago (A)
Most Stolen Bases, Game, Blue Jays	5, June 16, Boston (A)
	5, July 3, New York (H), 10 innings
Most Stolen Bases, Game, Opponents	4, May 23, Cleveland (A)
	4, May 26, Cleveland (A)
Most Stolen Bases, Inning, Blue Jays	3, 7th inning, June 16, Boston (A)
Most Stolen Bases, Inning, Opponents	2, 4 times
Most Doubles, Game, Blue Jays	** 7, July 21, Oakland (H)
Most Doubles, Game, Opponents	5, June 8, Detroit (H)
	5, June 14, Boston (A)
Most Triples, Game, Blue Jays	2, June 20, Boston (H)
	2, June 25, Milwaukee (H)
Most Triples, Game, Opponents	2, April 16, Texas (H)
	2, June 9, Detroit (H)
	2, September 18, Boston (A)
Most Left on Base, Blue Jays .	14, July 9, Seattle (A), 13 innings
Most Left on Base, Opponents	14, July 9, Seattle (A), 13 innings
	14, July 30, Baltimore (A), 10 innings

TEAM FIELDING

Most Double Plays, Game, Blue Jays	5, September 25, Boston (H), 13 innings
Most Double Plays, Game, Opponents	4, May 21, Chicago (H)
Most Errors, Game, Blue Jays	5, July 6, Oakland (A)
Most Errors, Game, Opponents	4, July 30, Baltimore (A)

TEAM PITCHING

Pitchers Most Strikeouts, Game, Blue Jays	**12, June 8, Detroit (H) **12, July 23, Seattle (H)
Pitchers Most Strikeouts, Game, Opponents	11, May 29, Chicago (A) 11, August 25, Chicago (A) 11, September 10, Detroit (H) 11, September 25, Boston (H), 13 innings
Pitchers Most Walks, Game, Blue Jays	11, July 30, Baltimore (A)
Pitchers Most Walks, Game, Opponents	7, May 26, Cleveland (A) 7, June 1, 1st game, Cleveland (H) 7, June 20, Boston (H) 7, August 18, Kansas City (H) 7, September 24, Boston (H)

INDIVIDUAL BATTING

Most Runs, Game	**4, Whitt, May 25, Cleveland (H)
Most Hits, Game	4, Barfield, May 3, Seattle (A) 4, Garcia, May 10, Seattle (H)

                                           4, Garcia, May 17,
                                              Minnesota (A)
                                           4, Mulliniks, April 14,
                                              Baltimore (A)
                                           4, Garcia, May 21, Chicago
                                              (H)
                                           4, Garcia, June 1, Cleveland
                                              (H)
                                           4, Matuszek, June 13,
                                              Boston (A)
                                           4, Upshaw, July 9, Seattle
                                              (A)
                                           4, Bell, September 28,
                                              Milwaukee (A)
                                           4, Fernandez, September 29,
                                              Milwaukee (A)

Most Doubles, Game . . . .   **3, Garcia, April 18, Texas
                                              (H)
Most Triples, Game . . . .   1, Many times
Most Home Runs, Game . . . .   2, Upshaw, April 28, Texas
                                              (A)
                                           2, Barfield, June 5,
                                              Minnesota (H)
                                           2, Barfield, July 31,
                                              Baltimore (A)
Most Runs Batted In, Game .   6, Garcia, May 10, Seattle
                                              (H)
Most Stolen Bases, Game . . .   2, Barfield (3), Garcia (1),
                                              Moseby (5), Bell (1)
Longest Hitting Streak . . . . . .   16, Barfield, May 8 - May 26
                                       16, Garcia, July 23 - Aug. 10
Grand Slam . . . . *2, Bell, July 9, Seattle (A)
                                              Bell, August 2, Texas (H)
                                           1, Whitt, June 23, Boston
                                              (H)

166

INDIVIDUAL PITCHING

Most Strikeouts, Game . . . . .   11, Alexander, July 23,
                                       Seattle (H)

Most Walks, Game . . . .   7, Stieb, September 12, New
                                       York (A)

Most Innings Game, Starter .   10, Key, June 6, Detroit (H)
Most Innings Game, Reliever   6, Lamp, May 4, Seattle (A)
Longest Winning Streak . . . . **11, Lamp (April 26 - Oct. 6)
Longest Losing Streak . . . . . .   4, Alexander, June 10 - July 6
                                    4, Caudill, May 15 -
                                    4, Lavelle, July 13 - July 30

Most Consecutive Scoreless
  Innings, Starter . . . .   *26, Stieb, May 17 - June 2
                                            (1st game), 8 IP

Most Consecutive Scoreless
  Innings, Reliever . . . .   Henke, 18.2 IP, July 29 -
                                         August 26

TEAM MISCELLANEOUS

Longest Winning Streak . . . .   *9, July 21 - 29
Longest Home Winning
  Streak . . . .   *10, July 21 - 28; August 2
                                            & 3

Longest Road Winning
  Streak . . . .   *7, April 14, April 26 - May 1
Longest Losing Streak . . . . . .   6, June 13 - 18
Longest Home Losing Streak   3, April 21 - 23
Longest Road Losing Streak .   6, June 13 - 18
Longest Game, Innings . . . . . 14, September 25, Milwaukee
                                     (H)

Longest Game, Time, Nine
  Innings . . . .   3:29, May 10, Seattle (H)

Longest Game, Time, Extra Innings	4:33, September 25, Boston (H), 13 innings
Fastest Game, Time	1:54, June 17, Milwaukee (A)
Largest Margin, Victory.....	10, May 22, Chicago (H), 10-0
	10, July 10, Seattle (A), 11-1
Largest Margin, Loss	12, September 18, Boston (A), 13-1
Largest Crowd, Exhibition Stadium.................	*47,686, October 4, New York (H)
Smallest Crowd, Exhibition Stadium.................	15,380, April 18, Texas
Largest Crowd, Road	54,699, September 15, New York
Smallest Crowd, Road	4,333, May 23, Cleveland
Biggest Deficit Overcome ...	4, April 19, Baltimore (H)
	4, June 20, Boston (H)
Biggest Lead Surrendered ...	6, May 17, Minnesota (A)

  * New Club Record
** Ties Club Record
(A) Away
(H) Home

168

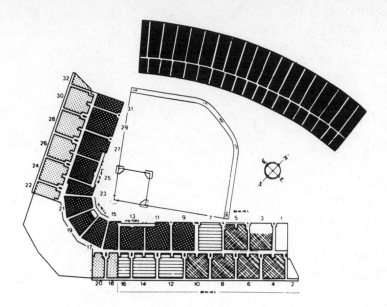

EXHIBITION STADIUM

CONSTRUCTED: 1975 - 76
OPENED: For baseball on April 7, 1977
SCOREBOARD: Electronic scoreboard built by Stewart-Warner, installed 1978 (41 feet high, 131 feet long).

Seating Capacity: 43,737

Playing Field Distances

Left Field	330	Centre Field	400
Left Centre	375	Right Centre	375
		Right Field	330

Height of Wall   12 feet
Turf: astroturf

TORONTO GROUND RULES
Exhibition Stadium

1. Foul poles are outside of the playing field. Any batted ball hitting foul pole above fence is a home run.
2. Ball sticking in the fence or padding, or going through wire screen in front of general admission stands — 2 Bases.
3. Ball remaining under or behind tarpaulin — out of play.
4. Ball going into bullpen bench and rebounding onto playing field — In Play
5. Ball hitting any portion of fence or screen in back of home plate — In Play
6. Ball hitting padding and bouncing over fence — 2 Bases.
7. A fairly batted or thrown ball that crosses the yellow line in front of the dugout's is considered in the dugout.

SOME FACTS ABOUT EXHIBITION STADIUM

- Capacity 43,737 for baseball and 53,816 for football.
- Monsanto Astroturf surface of 160,000 square feet is largest artificial playing surface in North America. New surface installed for 1985 season.
- Construction started in December 1974.
- Most of infield, including pitcher's mound, home plate, and first base, is located outside of football field area, allowing for permanent installation.
- Second and third base locations are convertible.
- Slope gradient of 1% for baseball and 2% for football.
- Chain-link outfield fence, 12 feet high, lower eight feet padded.
- Warning track made of textured synthetic Chevron.
- Distance from fair territory to out-of-play is 47 feet, 6 inches, at first base and third base, and 60 feet directly behind home plate to screen.
- 20 light standards, each 180 feet high, providing 250 foot-candles of illumination on the infield.
- Dugouts connected to clubhouses by tunnels, TV camera locations provided at end of dugouts.
- Height of stadium at outside wall behind home plate— 65 feet.
- 14 private club boxes, leased by Exhibition Stadium Corporation.
- Concessions operated by VS Services.
- Electronic scoreboard built by Stewart-Warner, installed 1978 (41 feet high, 131 feet long).

EXHIBITION STADIUM FIRSTS

GAME — Thurs., April 7, 1977 (Blue Jays 9, Chicago White Sox 5)

ATTENDANCE — 44,649

TIME/TEMP. — 3:22/0°C. (32°F).

PITCHER — Bill Singer, Toronto

BATTER — Ralph Garr, Chicago (walked)

PLATE UMPIRE — Nestor Chylak

PITCH — Called strike

HIT — Home run by Richie Zisk, first inning, one on

RUN — Ralph Garr (scored to Zisk's home run)

SINGLE — Jim Spencer, Chicago, April 7, 1977, first inning

DOUBLE — Richie Zisk, Chicago, April 7, 1977, second inning

TRIPLE — Ron LeFlore, Detroit, April 12, 1977, fifth inning

HOME RUN — Richie Zisk, April 7, 1977, first inning

FIRST RBI — Jorge Orta, Chicago, April 7, 1977, 1st inning

INSIDE-THE-PARK HOME RUN — Cecil Cooper, Milwaukee, May 5, 1977 (fifth inning)

GRAND SLAM HOME RUN — Hector Torres vs. New York, John 27, 1977 (fifth inning, off Ron Guidry)

TWO HOME-RUN GAME — Doug Ault, Toronto, April 7, 1977

THREE HOME-RUN GAME — John Mayberry, K.C., June 1, 1977

PINCH-HIT HOME RUN — Al Woods, Toronto, April 7, 1977 (fifth inning)

WINNING PITCHER — Jerry Johnson, Toronto (in relief), April 7, 1977

LOSING PITCHER — Ken Brett, Chicago (starter), April 7, 1977

SAVE — Pete Vuckovich, Toronto, April 7, 1977

PUTOUT — Steve Bowling, Toronto (fly ball to right field) April 7, 1977

ASSIST — Hector Torres, Toronto (ground ball to shortstop) April 7, 1977

ERROR — Rick Cerone, Toronto, April 7, 1977

SHUTOUT — Ferguson Jenkins, Boston, Sun. April 24, 1977 (9 - 0)

1985 BLUE JAYS DAY-BY-DAY

Date	Won/Lost	League Position	Games Behind	Opponent	Day/Night	Score	Winner	Loser
4-8	0-1	T5	1	@KC	D	L1-2	Black(1-0)	Stieb(0-1)
4-9	0-1	T4	1	OFF				
4-10	1-1	4	1	@KC	N	W1-0(10)	rCaudill(1-0)	rBeckwith(0-1)
4-11	2-1	4	1	@KC	N	W4-3(10)	rCaudill(2-0)	rQuisenberry(0-1)
4-12	2-2	5	1½	@BALT	N	L2-7	McGregor(1-0)	Key(0-1)
4-13	2-3	5	2½	@BALT	D	L7-8	rT.Martinez(1-0)	rCaudill(2-1)
4-14	3-3	5	2½	@BALT	D	W5-3	Alexander(1-0)	Boddicker(1-1)
4-15	3-3	5	2½	OFF				
4-16	3-4	6	3½	TEX	D	L4-9	Mason(1-1)	Leal(0-1)
4-17	4-4	4	2½	TEX	D	W3-1(10)	rCaudill(3-1)	rStewart(O-1)
4-18	5-4	5	2	TEX	D	W4-2	Stieb(1-1)	Tanana(0-2)
4-19	6-4	3	1	BALT	N	W6-5	Alexander(2-0)	rStewart(1-1)
4-20	7-4	2	1	BALT	D	W3-2	rMusselman(1-0)	rT.Martinez(1-2)
4-21	7-5	2	1	BALT	D	L2-3	D.Martinez(1-1)	Key(0-2)
4-22	7-6	3	1	KC	N	L0-2	Liebrandt(2-0)	Stieb(1-2)
4-23	7-7	T4	2	KC	N	L6-7	rBeckwith(1-1)	rCaudill(3-2)
4-24	8-7	5	1	KC	D	W10-2	Leal(1-1)	Saberhagen(1-2)
4-25	8-7	T4	1	OFF				

172

Date	Record	Pos	GB	Opp	D/N	Score	Winner	Loser
4-26	9-7	T3	1	@TEX	N	W6-5	rLamp(1-0)	rSchmidt(0-1)
4-27	10-7	T2	½	@TEX	N	W9-8(10)	rAcker(1-0)	rStewart(0-2)
4-28	11-7	T2	½	@TEX	D	W6-3	Alexander (3-0)	Mason(2-2)
4-29	12-7	2	—	@OAK	N	W2-1	Leal(2-1)	Krueger(2-2)
4-30	13-7	1	+½	@OAK	N	W4-3	rLamp(2-0)	rHowell(0-1)
5-1	14-7	1	+½	@CALF	N	W6-3	Key(1-2)	McCaskill(0-1)
5-2	14-8	1	—	@CALF	N	L2-3	rClements(2-0)	Stieb(1-3)
5-3	15-8	2	—	@SEA	N	W5-4	Alexander(4-0)	Barojas(0-3)
5-4	15-9	2	—	@SEA	N	L1-8	Young(2-3)	Leal(2-2)
5-5	15-10	2	1	@SEA	N	L1-4	Langston(4-2)	Clancy(0-1)
5-6	15-10	2	1	OFF				
5-7	16-10	2	1	OAK	N	W10-1	Stieb(2-3)	Sutton(2-3)
5-8	16-11	3	1	OAK	N	L4-6	McCatty(2-1)	Alexander(4-1)
5-9	16-11	3	1	OFF		PEARSON CUP		
5-10	17-11	3	1	SEA	N	W8-3	rKey(2-2)	Langston(4-3)
5-11	18-11	2	1	SEA	D	W4-2	rCaudill(4-2)	M.Young(2-4)
5-12	19-11	2	—	SEA	D	W9-5	Stieb(3-3)	Beattie(1-4)
5-13	19-11	1	+½	OFF				
5-14	20-11	1	+1	CALF	N	W6-3	Alexander(5-1)	Slaton(3-2)
5-15	20-12	1	+1	CALF	N	L6-9	rMoore(2-1)	rCaudill(4-3)
5-16	20-12	1	+1	OFF				
5-17	20-13	T1	—	@MINN	N	L6-7(11)	rFilson(1-0)	rLeal(2-3)
5-18	21-13	1	+½	@MINN	D	W3-1	Clancy(1-1)	Smithson(4-3)
5-19	21-14	T1	—	@MINN	D	L2-8	rFilson(2-0)	Alexander(5-2)
5-20	22-14	1	+½	CHGO	D	W6-1	Key(3-2)	Seaver(4-2)

Date	Won/Lost	League Position	Games Behind	Opponent	Day/Night	Score	Winner	Loser
5-21	23-14	1	+1½	CHGO	N	W4-3	rLavelle(1-0)	rJames(1-1)
5-22	24-14	1	+1½	CHGO	N	W10-0	Stieb(4-3)	Dotson(2-2)
5-23	25-14	1	+2½	@CLEV	N	W6-5	rLamp(3-0)	rWaddell(1-3)
5-24	26-14	1	+2½	@CLEV	N	W7-6	rLamp(4-0)	Creel(0-2)
5-25	27-14	1	+3	@CLEV	D	W10-7	rMusselman(2-0)	rThompson(1-2)
5-26	28-14	1	+3	@CLEV	D	W6-5	rLavelle(2-0)	rCreel(0-3)
5-27	28-14	1	+3½	@CHGO	D	PPD – – – RAIN RESCHEDULED		
5-28	29-14	1	+4	@CHGO	N	W6-1	Stieb(5-3)	Dotson(2-3)
5-29	29-15	1	+4	@CHGO	N	L5-8	Burns(6-4)	Clancy(1-2)
5-30	29-15	1	+3½	OFF				
5-31	30-15	1	+4	CLEV	N	W7-2	Alexander(6-2)	BClark(1-1)
6-1	31-15	1	+5	CLEV	D	W8-3	Key(4-2)	Blyleven (3-6)
6-2]	31-16	1	—	CLEV	TD-DH	L4-5	Heaton(4-4)	Stieb(5-4)
6-2]	32-16	1	+4½	CLEV	TD-DH	W5-2	Leal(3-3)	Behenna(0-1)
6-3	32-16	1	+4	OFF				
6-4	33-16	1	+5	MINN	N	W9-2	Clancy(2-2)	Viola(6-5)
6-5	34-16	1	+5	MINN	N	W5-0	Alexander(7-2)	Smithson(4-5)
6-6	35-16	1	+5½	DET	N	W2-0(12)	r.Acker(2-0)	rLopez(0-4)
6-7	36-16	1	+6½	DET	N	W9-2	Stieb(6-4)	Terrell(6-2)
6-8	36-17	1	+6½	DET	D	L1-10	O'Neal(1-0)	Leal(3-4)
6-9	35-18	1	+6½	DET	D	L3-8	Bair(1-0)	Clancy(2-3)
6-10	36-19	1	+5½	@NY	N	L2-4	Shirley(1-1)	Alexander(7-3)
6-11	37-19	1	+6	@NY	N	W4-1(11)	rLamp(5-0)	rFisher(2-1)

Date	Record	Games	Home/Away	Result	D/N	Winning Pitcher	Losing Pitcher
6-12	38-19	1	+6	@NY	W3-2(10)	N	rAcker(3-0)	rBordi(1-1)
6-13	38-20	1	+5½	@BOS	L7-8	N	rTrujillo(1-1)	rLavelle(2-1)
6-14	38-21	1	+4½	@BOS	L1-4	N	Boyd(8-4)	Clancy(2-4)
6-15	38-22	1	+3½	@BOS	L5-7	D	rStanley(2-2)	rAcker(3-1)
6-16	38-23	1	+3½	@BOS	L6-7	D	rCrawford(4-2)	rLavelle(2-2)
6-17	38-24	1	+2½	@MILW	L1-2	N	Haas(6-3)	Stieb(6-5)
6-18	38-25	1	+2½	@MILW	L1-4	N	Burris(4-5)	Leal(3-5)
6-19	39-25	1	+2½	@MILW	W5-1	D	Clancy(3-4)	Vuckovich(2-5)
6-20	40-25	1	+2½	BOS	W6-5	N	rAcker(4-1)	rStanley(2-3)
6-21	41-25	1	+2½	BOS	W7-2	N	Key(5-2)	Hurst(2-7)
6-22	41-26	1	+2½	BOS	L3-5	D	rStanley(3-3)	rAcker(4-2)
6-23	42-26	1	+2½	BOS	W8-1	D	Stieb(7-5)	Kison(3-2)
6-24	42-26	1	+3	OFF				
6-25	43-26	1	+3	MILW	W7-1	N	Clancy(4-4)	Burris(4-6)
6-26	43-27	1	+2	MILW	L4-5	N	rGibson(6-4)	Alexander(7-4)
6-27	44-27	1	+2½	MILW	W7-3	N	Key(6-2)	Higuera(4-5)
6-28	45-27	1	+3½	@DET	W2-0	N	Stieb(8-5)	Petry(9-6)
6-29	45-28	1	+2½	@DET	L0-8	N	Terrell(9-3)	Leal(3-6)
6-30	46-28	1	+3½	@DET	W6-5	D	rLavelle(3-2)	rLopez(1-5)
7-1	46-29	1	+2½	NY	L1-4	D	Cowley(7-3)	Alexander(7-5)
7-2	46-30	1	+2½	NY	L3-5	N	Whitson(4-6)	Key(6-3)
7-3	47-30	1	+2½	NY	W3-2(10)	D	rAcker(5-2)	rBordi(1-2)
7-4	47-31	1	+2½	@OAK	L2-3	N	rHowell(8-3)	rCaudill(4-4)
7-5	48-31	1	+3½	@OAK	W8-2	N	Clancy(5-4)	Krueger(5-8)
7-6	48-32	1	+2½	@OAK		D		

Date	Won/Lost	League Position	Games Behind	Opponent	Day/Night	Score	Winner	Loser
7-7	49-32	1	+2½	@OAK	D	L1-5	Sutton(8-5)	Alexander(7-6)
7-8	50-32	1	+3½	@SEA	N	W8-2	Key(7-3)	McCatty(4-4)
7-9	51-32	1	+3½	@SEA	N	W4-0	Stieb(9-5)	Moore(7-5)
7-10	52-32	1	+3½	@SEA	N	W9-4(13)	rMusselman(3-0)	rVandeBerg(0-1)
7-11	53-32	1	+4½	@CALF	N	W11-1	Clancy(6-4)	Wills(4-2)
7-12	53-33	1	+4½	@CALF	N	W5-3	Alexander(8-6)	Slaton(4-8)
7-13	53-34	1	+3½	@CALF	N	L3-5	McCaskill(5-5)	Key(7-4)
7-14	53-35	1	+2½	@CALF	D	L3-4	Witt(7-6)	rLavelle(3-3)
7-15)						L3-5	rCliburn(4-2)	rLavelle(3-4)
7-16								
7-17)								

* * * * * ALL-STAR BREAK * * * * * *

Date	Won/Lost	League Position	Games Behind	Opponent	Day/Night	Score	Winner	Loser
7-18	53-36	1	+2½	OAK	N	L4-6	rOntiveros(1-1)	rLavelle(3-5)
7-19	54-36	1	+2½	OAK	N	W5-1	Key(8-4)	Sutton(9-6)
7-20	54-37	1	+1½	OAK	D	L1-5	Birtsas(6-2)	Stieb(9-6)
7-21	55-37	1	+1½	OAK	D	W11-4	rLamp(6-0)	Krueger(7-9)
7-22	56-37	1	+2½	SEA	N	W3-1	Filer(1-0)	Langston(5-7)
7-23	57-37	1	+3½	SEA	N	W4-2	Alexander(9-6)	Moore(8-6)
7-24	58-37	1	+4½	SEA	N	W3-1	Key(9-4)	Young(7-11)
7-25	59-37	1	+5	CALF	N	W7-0	Stieb(10-6)	Witt(8-7)
7-26	60-37	1	+6	CALF	N	W8-3	Clancy(7-4)	Lugo(3-3)
7-27	61-37	1	+6	CALF	D	W8-3	Filer(2-0)	Mack(0-1)
7-28	62-37	1	+7	CALF	N	W5-1	Alexander(10-6)	McCaskill(6-7)
7-29	63-37	1	+7	@BALT	N	W4-3(10)	rHenke(1-0)	Boddicker(10-11)

176

Date	Record	Pos	GB	Opp	N/D	Result	Pitcher	Pitcher
7-30	63-38	1	+6½	@BALT	N	L3-4(10)	rAase(6-5)	rLavelle(3-6)
7-31	64-38	1	+7½		N	W5-3	rHenke(2-0)	D.Martinez(7-7)
8-1	65-38	1	+8½	@BALT	N	W9-3	Filer(3-0)	Davis(5-7)
8-2	66-38	1	+9½	TEX	N	W5-3	Alexander(11-6)	Cook(2-3)
8-3	67-38	1	+9½	TEX	D	W4-1	rLamp(7-0)	Welsh(2-3)
8-4	67-39	1	+9½	TEX	D	L4-8	Hough(10-11)	Stieb(10-7)
8-5	67-39	1	+9	OFF				
8-6]								
8-7]								

* * * * STRIKE * * * *

Date	Record	Pos	GB	Opp	N/D	Result	Pitcher	Pitcher
8-8]	68-39	1	—	BALT	TN-DH	W7-2	Alexander(12-6)	McGregor(9-9)
8-8]	69-39	1	+9	BALT	TN-DH	W7-4	Filer(4-0)	Boddicker(10-13)
8-9	69-40	1	+8	@KC	N	L2-4	Black(8-11)	Stieb(10-8)
8-10	69-41	1	+7	@KC	N	L3-4(10)	rQuisenberry(6-6)	rCaudill(4-5)
8-11	70-41	1	+7	@KC	D	W5-3(10)	rHenke(3-0)	rBeckwith(1-5)
8-12	70-42	1	+6	@TEX	N	L4-5	rHenry(1-0)	rCaudill(4-6)
8-13	71-42	1	+7	@TEX	N	W5-3	Filer(5-0)	Russell(0-2)
8-14	72-42	1	+7	@TEX	N	W4-1	Stieb(11-8)	Hough(11-12)
8-15	72-42	1	+7	OFF				
8-16	72-43	1	+6	KC	N	L2-4	Liebrandt(11-6)	Key(9-5)
8-17	72-44	1	+5	KC	D	L2-4	Jackson(11-7)	Alexander(12-7)
8-18	73-44	1	+5	KC	D	W10-6	Filer(6-0)	Gubicza(9-7)
8-19	73-45	1	+4	@CLEV	N	L3-5	Waddell(6-5)	Stieb(11-9)
8-20	74-45	1	+4	@CLEV	N	W3-2	Key(10-5)	Smith(1-1)
8-21	74-46	1	+3	@CLEV	N	L2-5	Heaton(7-13)	Alexander(12-8)
8-22	74-46	1	+3½	OFF				

Date	Won/Lost	League Position	Games Behind	Opponent	Day/Night	Score	Winner	Loser
8-23]	75-46	1	—	@CHGO	TN-DH	W6-3	Filer(7-0)	Burns(13-8)
8-23[	76-46	1	+4	@CHGO	TN-DH	W10-3	rAcker(6-2)	Nelson(7-8)
8-24	77-46	1	+4	@CHGO	N	W6-3	Stieb(12-9)	Seaver(12-9)
8-25	77-47	1	+3	@CHGO	D	L3-5	Bannister(6-11)	Key(10-6)
8-26	78-47	1	+4	@MINN	N	W4-3	Alexander(13-8)	Blyleven(12-13)
8-27	79-47	1	+5	@MINN	N	W8-0	rDavis(1-0)	Viola(13-11)
8-28	79-48	1	+4½	@MINN	D	L5-6(10)	rFilson(4-5)	rHenke(3-1)
8-29	79-48	1	+4	OFF				
8-30	80-48	1	+5	CHGO	N	W5-3	Key(11-6)	Bannister(6-12)
8-31	81-48	1	+5	CHGO	D	W6-2	rLavelle(4-6)	J.Davis(1-2)
9-1	81-49	1	+4	CHGO	D	L1-4	Burns(15-8)	S.Davis(1-1)
9-2	82-49	1	+4	CHGO	D	W3-2	Stieb(13-9)	Wardle(6-6)
9-3	82-49	1	+3½	OFF				
9-4	82-50	1	+2½	CLEV	N	L4-5	rClark(2-3)	rHenke(3-2)
9-5	83-50	1	+2½	MINN	N	W7-0	Alexander(14-8)	Blyleven(13-14)
9-6	84-50	1	+2½	MINN	N	W8-3	Davis(2-1)	Viola(13-13)
9-7	84-51	1	+1½	MINN	D	L3-6	Smithson(14-11)	Stieb(13-10)
9-8	85-51	1	+1½	MINN	D	W10-9	rLamp(8-0)	Portugal(1-2)
9-9	86-51	1	+1½	DET	N	W5-3	Key(12-6)	Mahler(0-1)
9-10	87-51	1	+1½	DET	N	W2-1	Alexander(15-8)	Morris(14-10)
9-11	88-51	1	+2½	DET	N	W3-2	rLamp(9-0)	Terrell(13-9)
9-12	88-52	1	+1½	@NT	N	L5-7	Guidry(19-5)	rLavelle(4-7)
9-13	89-52	1	+2½	@NY	N	W3-2	rLavelle(5-7)	Niekro(15-10)
9-14	90-52	1	+3½	@NY	N	W7-4	Key(13-6)	rBordi(5-7)

9-15	91-52	1	+4½	@NY	D	W8-5	Alexander(16-8)	Whitson(10-8)
9-16	91-52	1	+5	OFF				
9-17	91-53	1	+5	@BOS	N	L5-6	Boyd(14-11)	Stieb(13-11)
9-18	91-54	1	+5	@BOS	N	L1-13	Nipper(9-11)	Clancy(7-5)
9-19	92-54	1	+5½	OFF				
9-20	92-54	1	+6½	MILW	N	W7-5	Key(14-6)	Cocanower(4-7)
9-21	93-54	1	+6½	MILW	N	W2-1(14)	rLamp(10-0)	rDarwin(7-18)
9-22	93-55	1	+5½	MILW	D	L1-2	Higuera(14-7)	Stieb(13-12)
9-23	94-55	1	+6	MILW	N	W5-1	Clancy(8-5)	Leary(1-2)
9-24	95-55	1	+7	BOS	N	W6-2	rLamp(11-0)	Nipper(9-12)
9-25	95-56	1	+6	BOS	N	L2-4(13)	rCrawford(6-4)	rCerutti(0-1)
9-26	95-57	1	+5½	BOS	N	L1-4	Sellers(2-0)	Alexander(16-9)
9-27	96-57	1	+6	@MILW	N	W5-1	Stieb(14-12)	Higuera(14-8)
9-28	97-57	1	+6	@MILW	N	W6-1	Clancy(9-5)	Leary(1-3)
9-29	98-57	1	+5½	@MILW	D	W13-5	rAcker(7-2)	Burris(9-13)
9-30	98-57	1	+5	OFF				
10-1	98-58	1	+4	@DET	N	L1-6	Tanana(11-14)	Alexander(16-10)
10-2	98-59	1	+4	@DET	N	L2-4	Morris(16-11)	Stieb(14-13)
10-3	98-60	1	+3	@DET	N	L0-2	Terrell(15-10)	Clancy(9-6)
10-4	98-61	1	+2	NY	N	L3-4	rScurry(1-0)	rHenke(3-3)
10-5	99-61	1	+3	NY	D	W5-1	Alexander(17-10)	Cowley(12-6)
10-6	99-62	1	+2	NY	D	L0-8	Niekro(16-12)	Cerutti(0-2)

r in relief